COOKING THE COWBOY WAY

ALSO BY
GRADY SPEARS
WITH JUNE NAYLOR

The Texas Cowboy Kitchen

COOKING THE COWBOY WAY

RECIPES INSPIRED BY CAMPFIRES, CHUCK WAGONS, AND RANCH KITCHENS

GRADY SPEARS

with **June Naylor and Kelly Frazier**

Foreword by **Colman Andrews**

Photography by **David Manning**

Andrews McMeel Publishing, LLC

Kansas City · Sydney · London

COOKING THE COWBOY WAY

Andrews McMeel Publishing, LLC

an Andrews McMeel Universal company

1130 Walnut Street, Kansas City, Missouri 64106

www.andrewsmcmeel.com

11 12 13 SDB 10 9 8 7 6 5 4 3

Library of Congress Cataloging-in-Publication Data

Spears, Grady.
  Cooking the cowboy way : recipes inspired by campfires, chuck wagons, and ranch kitchens / Grady Spears with June Naylor ; foreword by Colman Andrews ; photography by David Manning.
     p. cm.
   ISBN: 978-0-7407-7392-1
  1. Cookery, American–Southwestern style. 2. Cookery, American–Western style. 3. Cookery–Texas. 4. Cowboys–United States. I. Naylor, June. II. Title.
   TX715.2.S69S697 2009
   641.59764--dc22

2009009323

Design by Diane Marsh

www.gradyspears.com

ATTENTION: SCHOOLS AND BUSINESSES
Andrews McMeel books are available at quantity discounts with bulk purchase for educational, business, or sales promotional use. For information, please e-mail the Andrews McMeel Publishing Special Sales Department:
specialsales@amuniversal.com

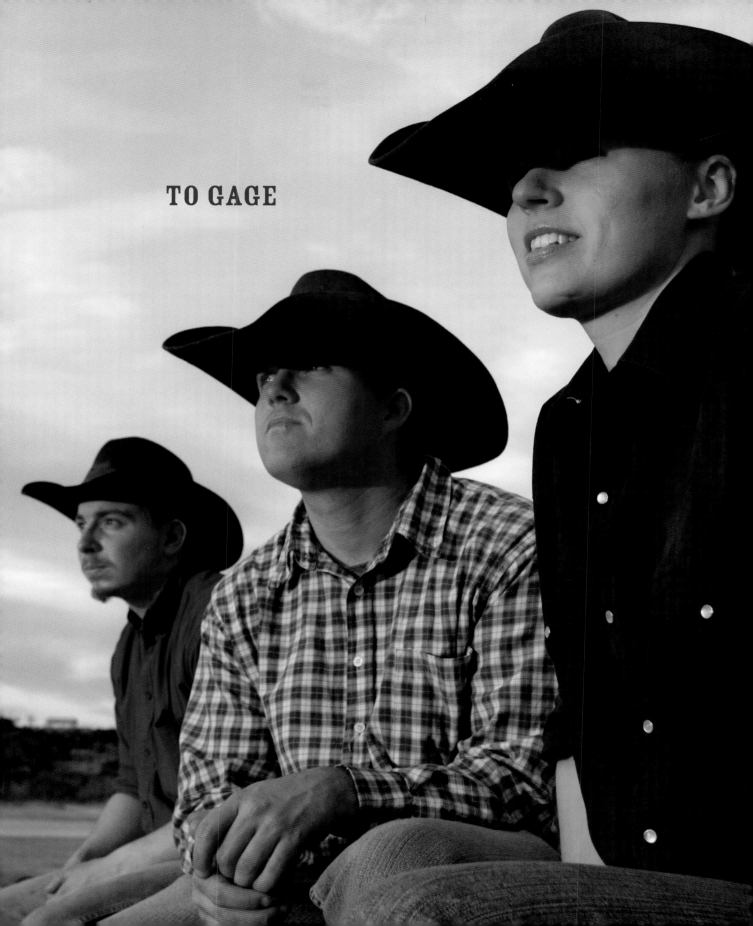

TO GAGE

CONTENTS

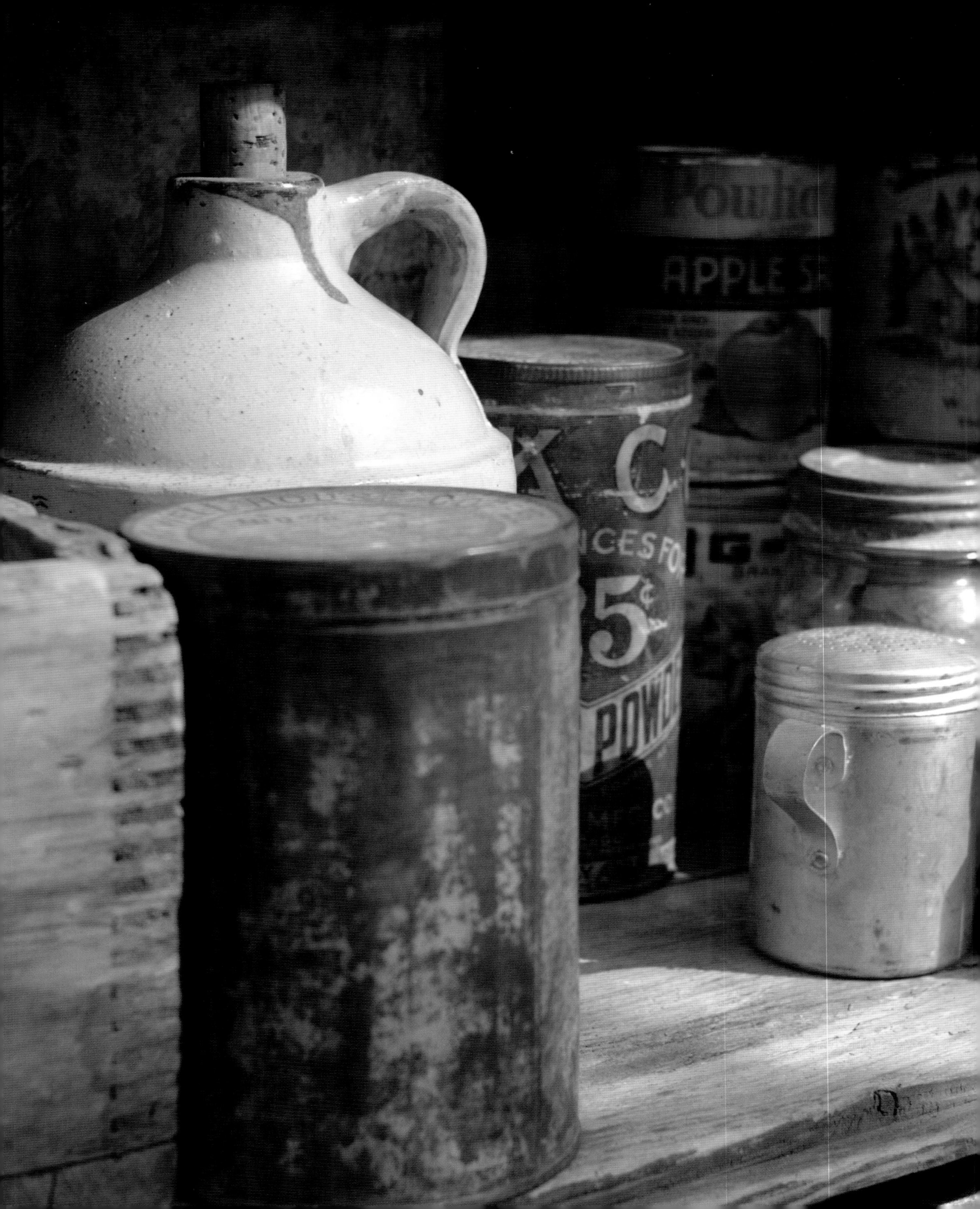
APPLE

ACKNOWLEDGMENTS

THERE ARE DOZENS OF generous souls who helped make our cross-continental journeys for the research and production of this book possible. We're forever grateful for the time, hospitality, enthusiasm, and wonderful food shared with us by Bob and Sonja Bratcher and Anne Skipper at the Wildcatter Ranch; Marty and Mary Margaret Richter at the Edwards Ranch; Terry Chandler and Bulldog McLeroy, Jim Wiginton and Bo Powell from Fred's Texas Café; Amy Smith and Fort Worth's Sweethearts of the Rodeo; Lisa and Tom Perini from Perini Ranch Steakhouse; Veronica and Richard Schultz and Ann Sullivan at Rancho de la Osa; Judy Love Rondeau and Alberta Tourism; Rob and Marci Matthews in Calgary; Mac Makenny and Brad McCarthy at Homeplace Ranch, near Banff; Diana Pfaff at the Irving Convention and Visitors Bureau; John and Gina Puente Brancato at La Buena Vida Vineyards in Grapevine; David and Susan Bellamy and Howard and Jennifer Bellamy in Darby; John, Taunia, and Ashlyn Elick at Texas Ranch Life; Laren Mahoney and the Kansas City Convention and Visitors Association; Carolyn Wells and the Kansas City Barbecue Society; Tim Keegan and Case Dorman at Fiorella's Jack Stack in Kansas City; Arzelia Gates and Mr. Ollie Gates at Gates Bar-B-Q in Kansas City; Louis Lambert at Lambert's Fort Worth; Billito and Kathy Donnell in Alpine; and Colleen Hodson and the Dude Ranchers' Association.

Out infinite gratitude goes to the many who made the idea work in the first place. We want to thank Kelly Frazier and Brian Mac, as well as Sia Antunues and the unbelievable, magical Lisa Ekus. At Andrews McMeel, we are grateful for the steady guidance and deep wisdom shared with us by Jean Lucas, Tim Lynch, and Kirsty Melville.

We owe a world of thanks to Dr. Anne VanBeber, chair of the Department of Nutritional Sciences at Texas Christian University in Fort Worth, and to her students, Denise Bennett, Melissa Cossich, Tom Davies, David Fishel, Candice George, Jaclyn Gomez, Jordan Hamon, Ryan Hamon, Carrie Hoover, Stephanie Isak, Katelyn Kelly, June Lietz, Nick LoPresti, Celeste Manner-McDade, Brittani Mincher, Katy Murray, Kirk Oliver, Emily Paper, Jessica Petersen, Stali Riley, Jennifer Salim, Crystal Sherman, Brett Singer, Cynthia Spurgat, Elizabeth Staples, Dylan Taylor-Smith, and Thuy Tran. Without their tireless help, we might never have finished testing recipes. Their sharp instincts and grounded cooking sensibilities kept us in line.

And at home, a world of heartfelt thanks to David Manning, who entertained us while shooting his heart out, and Dawnne Manning, who generously loaned her husband's time; Richard and Barbara Chowning, who kept doggies happy and home fires burning; Barbara Rodriguez and Meda Kessler, who gave us the right words when we couldn't find any that worked; and Jen and Gage, whose love and patience made everything worthwhile.

FOREWORD

BY COLMAN ANDREWS

I KNEW A LOT OF COWBOYS when I was a kid. They were on TV every afternoon. Like most young American males back in the mid-twentieth century, I admired cowboys; they were my early role models. They rode horses and wore cool clothes, after all. They always outdrew the bad guys. And they didn't put up with any mushy stuff from girls. Sure, the dramatic depictions of the Old West that my generation grew up with were corny and inaccurate, but they gave us heroes who were heroic for reasons that had nothing to do with knowing how to track a miscreant by his DNA or how to destroy a terrorist stronghold with Semtex. Cowboys were hardworking, independent, courageous, and honest. They did what was right, even when it wasn't easy. They did what a man's gotta do.

Then some short guy with an apron and a funny hat would clang on a big iron triangle and yell, "Come and git it!"

What was it that they came and got? Even back then, I had food on my mind, but there weren't many clues around the old TV chuck wagon. Apart from an occasional joke about beans or biscuits, the subject just never seemed to come up.

I'm pretty sure, though, that my early cowboy heroes weren't eating anything as good as the victuals described by Grady Spears in this richly textured, wonderfully appetite-inducing volume. Spears, who has worked as a cowboy (and also as a serious chef), has drawn recipes and inspiration from cooks on and around ranches all over his native Texas and beyond—even from cattle country in Florida and Canada. Some of this food is hardy, savory, down-home stuff— Tom Perini's Chuck Wagon Stew, Smoke-Braised Short Ribs, Mom's Yellow Butter Cupcakes—while some is, well, more inspired. (Did Randolph Scott ever sample maple balsamic vinaigrette? Would John Wayne have been caught dead eating crème brûlée with white chocolate chips?) Everything herein is cowboy honest, though—the kind of fare that any hardworking, independent, courageous, modern-day wrangler, even a wrangler of office files or Junior's soccer team, would be mighty glad to come and git.

THE COWBOY WAY

RECIPES INSPIRED BY CAMPFIRES, CHUCK WAGONS, AND RANCH KITCHENS

GROWING UP IN TEXAS, I dreamed of one day being a cowboy.

When I got to high school, I got lucky; instead of football and hot rods, I got to spend time working with cattle. This wasn't just a passing experience; from then on, I was hooked on the cowboy way of life that, in some ways, has changed little over the years. I'd always respected the men and women who made their living from long days in the saddle, but once I'd walked in their boots, I understood the uniqueness of life on the trail. And because tastes and smells can transport you back in time, I've used my cooking to reach back to this cowboy experience ever since I first lived it.

The cowboy's world has been idealized in film and books, but the real cowboy's life is far from glamorous. In spite of how much we've painted it with romantic strokes, he doesn't choose his line of work expecting to lead a charmed life framed in those

famous Roy Rogers sunsets. Willie Nelson immortalized this idea in his song "My Heroes Have Always Been Cowboys," singing of the cowboys' loneliness and the dreams that keep them a separate pace from the rest of the world.

Few folks understand that a real cowboy lives by a code defined by respect for hard work, an understanding of the rhythms of nature, and—you can't overlook this—an appreciation for honest food. Long days outdoors in every kind of weather, sometimes for weeks at a time, make a cowboy's hunger a challenge for ranch cooks from Texas to Florida, north into Canada, and south of the border to the *caballeros* in Mexico and the gauchos in South America. Even the *paniolos* in Hawaii fill up on foods that cast-iron cooks through the ages have provided not just as fuel for aching bodies, but as a sort of spiritual nutrition that gives meaning to the expression "comfort food."

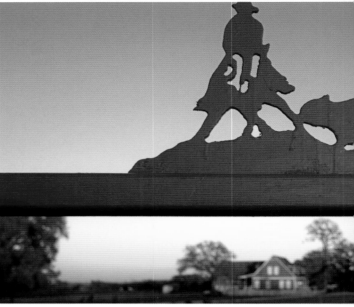

Life in the saddle, on the trail or in the outback, has forged a style of living that I call the Cowboy Way. It's a life where boots and hats are always about function, not fashion. It means that when you eat, drink, and breathe the tending of cattle, the raising of beef is not just some exercise where loss is charted on a spreadsheet. When your days are filled with the smell of fresh-cut hay and the creaking of worn leather, when you wake up with the sun and to the smell of coffee on the boil and biscuits from the chuck wagon, you are living the Cowboy Way.

. . . WHEN YOU WAKE UP WITH THE SUN AND TO THE SMELL OF COFFEE ON THE BOIL AND BISCUITS FROM THE CHUCK WAGON, YOU ARE LIVING THE COWBOY WAY.

Some of the most valuable lessons I learned—about food and about life—came from cowboy cooks whose workdays extended from well before sun-up till way past sundown. From wranglers and cooks like Brad McCarthy on the Homeplace Ranch, just outside of Calgary, I learned that the cooking that pleases a cowboy will please regular folks, too. As Brad says, most people just want regular food, the comforting stuff, not plates that are gussied up the way a lot of formally trained chefs learned to do. When you experience his Shepherd's Pie (page 99) and Ranch Potato Pancakes (page 103), you'll see he knows a lot about pleasing cowboys and anybody else who eats.

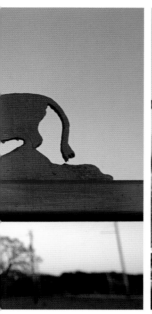

Cowboy cooks have a lot in common with the men and women they feed. As Terry Chandler, a Fort Worth café owner who is also the chuck wagon cook for the historic 6666 Ranch in West Texas, says, working cattle and doing his kind of cooking are "all about want-to." Both cowboys and chuck wagon cooks do what they do strictly for the love of the job, because neither are in danger of getting rich in their work.

To meet and work with folks like Brad and Terry was a major motivation for me to write *The Cowboy Way*. This collection of recipes is the result of a journey I've also shared in these pages, a journey through Texas and North America, but also a journey through history. I think whether you simply read this book or cook from it, like me, you'll be carried away by the magic of starry nights by the campfire and seduced by the heritage of the chuck wagon and ranch kitchens where the menus are still stoked by the traditions of the Old West, just as they have been for a hundred years or more.

In these pages you'll have a ringside seat at the rodeo, as I wrestle down new recipes from some incredible cowboy cooks and kitchen wranglers who know what hungry cowfolks want to eat. Some recipes are my own, and others have been adapted from cooks you'll meet as we journey. Some recipes were too perfect for me to tamper with; the good flavors and time-tested techniques speak for themselves.

Always the food I've included here spoke to me of honesty, resourcefulness, and the integrity of the land, as well as the goodness of the people who depend on that land. But I've also tried to capture something special from those meals, which were as unique and powerful as the rose-colored sunsets

and cactus-filled vistas at places like Rancho de la Osa near Tucson. Riding a horse across the Sonoran Desert there made me expect the famous old Hollywood cowboy Tom Mix, who visited the ranch back in the day, to come racing over the mountain on his horse at any moment. When I wasn't cooking with the ranch chef, Ann, or mixing it up over tequila in the cantina with guests, I heard fascinating stories from ranch owners Veronica and Richard about the famous politicians and writers who filled the guest books through the years.

Those stories join the ones from Florida ranchers and country-music singers the Bellamy Brothers, who schooled me on the cattle-ranching heritage of the coastal prairies and other tropical Cowboy Way ideas down south. It was the Bellamy Brothers who taught me (as we cooked together) that beyond Disney World, glitzy South Beach, and Daytona's racetracks, Florida has a 500-year-old cattle industry that helps drive the state economy. In fact, the state's total breeding herd is worth nearly $850 million. The cowboys who run cattle over Florida's 4 million acres of pastureland have been fed by honest cookery like the Bellamys' own steaks and citrus for centuries.

I made discoveries of a different culinary sort in Kansas City, nicknamed "Cowtown" like my home city of Fort Worth. It's not a secret that Kansas City is famous for what may be the most popular cowboy food of all time–barbecue–but in these pages you'll learn, as I did, that barbecue goes way beyond the pork ribs and beef brisket everyone expects. Whatever they can put their hands on, Kansas City folks will barbecue, from lamb and wild game

to fish, just as cowboys roasted whatever they could throw on their fires back in the cattle-driving days.

Back home in Texas, I spent plenty of time in the saddle and at the cook-stove collecting stories and recipes to share from Buffalo Gap to Big Bend. Whether gathering recipes from cowboy cooks at tailgate parties or trying to keep up the pace at wild 'n' woolly chuck wagon brunches with the likes of the Outlaw Chef and the Sweethearts of the Rodeo, my goal was to document a celebration of open spaces and the big hearts of a people as well as the food they love, from the Outlaw Chef's Sourdough Biscuits with Green Chile Cream Gravy to Ranchero Grilled Quail with Vaqueros Migas.

I didn't think much about the philosophy of cowboy cooking when I started my journey. I just knew it felt right and tasted good. But when I started thinking about collecting recipes from the cooks who fuel life in the Cowboy Way, I came to understand that in addition to cooking tips and recipes, these folks had passed along to me timeless wisdom and skills that help me love cooking more than ever, even when I'm spending more time surrounded by stainless steel appliances than under the starry skies. Maybe you'll find you need the kind of reassurance that food from rustic life brings; maybe the stress of our modern-day world will have you reaching for a little romance of a yesteryear hero and the comfort of chow that never goes out of style. If so, I think these recipes and stories will transport you, too, back to the simpler, Cowboy Way of life.

WILDCATTER RANCH

GRAHAM, TEXAS

THE WILDCATTER RANCH IS A 1,500-ACRE SPREAD ON THE RANCH LAND JUST OUTSIDE OF GRAHAM, AN OLD TOWN NEAR THE BEAUTIFUL POSSUM KINGDOM LAKE, AND ABOUT NINETY MINUTES NORTHWEST OF MY HOME IN FORT WORTH. THE RANCH SITS IN THE WIDE UPPER BRAZOS RIVER VALLEY AND HAS VIEWS OF THE WOODED, ROCKY COUNTRYSIDE THAT PITCHES AND ROLLS TOWARD THE SOUTH AND WEST. CLOSE BY IS THE PLACE WHERE THE CATTLE RAISERS ASSOCIATION WAS FOUNDED IN 1877 TO REGULATE RANCHING AND PUT AN END TO CATTLE RUSTLING.

AFTER SUPPER, YOU CAN SIT IN A ROCKER

ON THE PORCH OF YOUR CABIN AND LISTEN TO

THE COYOTES' NIGHT CALLS . . .

The Wildcatter is well known for fantastic food, thanks to Bob Bratcher, a good ol' cowboy chef who comes from the West Texas town of Seymour and has a real passion for the Cowboy Way. Bob gave up a sales job because he loved cooking so much; he cooked for parties and big groups, and eventually became the head cook at the Wildcatter. Since then, Bob the Cook– that's what all the ranch folks call him–has won awards for his ribs, and his food at the Wildcatter Steakhouse was named among the state's best by *Texas Monthly* magazine.

Bob and I like the same kind of cooking, such as putting really good, spicy rubs on everything from steaks and ribs to chicken and game. If you go eat at the Wildcatter, be sure and get a table by the windows, where you can look out across limestone bluffs crowned with brushy live oaks at a purple-and-orange sunset when you cut into one of Bob's phenomenal porterhouse steaks, with a side of his crazy-rich creamed spinach. For dessert, you won't regret having the buttermilk pound cake, one of the best I've ever tasted, made from his mom's recipe. And you'll be able to make all of these at home, following recipes in the next few pages.

The cowboy lifestyle and the big meals will make you want to stick around the Wildcatter awhile. Because the ranch owners found that nobody wanted to go home after eating Bob's cooking, they built some cabins for overnight stays. After supper, you can sit in a rocker on the porch of your cabin and listen to the coyotes' night calls, and in the morning you can sit there with your coffee, planning your day of horseback riding and canoeing as you look out over the horseshoe bends that the Brazos River cuts on its way toward the south valley. Me, I'll just be plotting to eat another one of Bob's unforgettable dinners or making plans to join him in the saloon at day's end. Both are essential parts of the Wildcatter's Cowboy Way, as the cowboy always dreams of a good steak and a cold beer when the work is done.

WILD MUSTANG SALAD

SERVES 8

This salad is one of my favorites, and it's just the right thing to go alongside a big ol' juicy steak. You can use pecans or walnuts, but the pistachios add good variety. Watch and make sure the nuts don't burn while they're in the oven. And when making the dressing, remember that using a good-quality, aged balsamic vinegar is the key.

8 cups spring mix or baby field greens

1½ cups Spicy Pistachios (recipe follows)

8 ounces blue cheese crumbles

8 strips crisp bacon, crumbled

¾ cup Maple-Balsamic Vinaigrette (recipe follows)

SPICY PISTACHIOS

2 cups shelled raw pistachios

2 tablespoons unsalted butter, melted

1 tablespoon Tabasco sauce

2 teaspoons Worcestershire sauce

1 teaspoon garlic powder

1 teaspoon paprika

1 teaspoon cayenne pepper

1½ teaspoons sea salt

To make the nuts, preheat the oven to 250°F. Line a baking sheet with parchment paper. Place all the ingredients in a large bowl and toss them together until the nuts are coated. Transfer to the baking sheet, and arrange them in a single layer. Bake, stirring every 15 minutes, until the pistachios are nicely toasted. Total baking time should be about 45 minutes. Remove the nuts from the oven and loosen them with a metal spatula. Let them cool on the pan.

MAPLE-BALSAMIC VINAIGRETTE

1 cup extra-virgin olive oil

2 tablespoons red wine vinegar

2 tablespoons aged balsamic vinegar

1½ tablespoons pure maple syrup

1 teaspoon Dijon mustard

Kosher salt and freshly ground black pepper

To make the vinaigrette, whisk all the ingredients together in a small bowl and adjust the seasonings to taste. Stored in an airtight container in the refrigerator, it will keep for 3 to 4 days.

To prepare the salad, place the greens in a bowl and top with the Spicy Pistachios, blue cheese, and bacon. Drizzle with the vinaigrette. Toss and serve immediately.

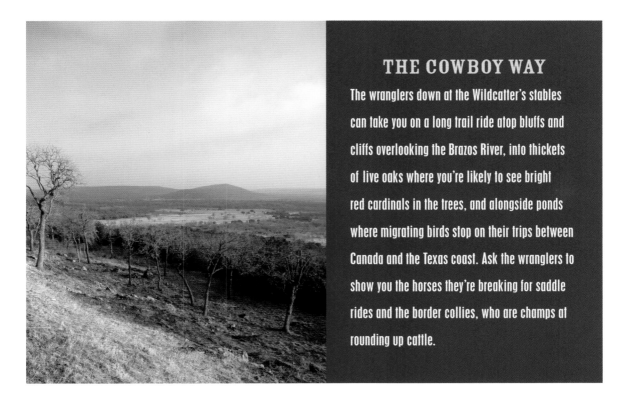

THE COWBOY WAY

The wranglers down at the Wildcatter's stables can take you on a long trail ride atop bluffs and cliffs overlooking the Brazos River, into thickets of live oaks where you're likely to see bright red cardinals in the trees, and alongside ponds where migrating birds stop on their trips between Canada and the Texas coast. Ask the wranglers to show you the horses they're breaking for saddle rides and the border collies, who are champs at rounding up cattle.

GRILLED SALMON WITH BARBECUE SAUCE

SERVES 6

If you think you've had good salmon, wait until you try it like Bob makes it at the Wildcatter. Although this doesn't seem like a usual fit for cowboy cooking, you may be surprised at how the barbecue sauce and the grill turn this fish into a hearty, satisfying supper.

3 pounds salmon fillets

3 cups Barbecue Sauce for Fish (recipe follows)

Place the salmon fillets in a long glass dish and cover with 1½ cups of the barbecue sauce. Cover the dish with plastic wrap and allow the fillets to marinate in the refrigerator for 2 hours. Remove them from the refrigerator 30 minutes before grilling time. Discard the marinade before cooking the fish.

Prepare coals or a gas grill to medium heat. Oil the grate so the fish won't stick. Place the marinated salmon fillets on the grill and cook for 6 to 8 minutes per side; baste with ½ cup of the barbecue sauce during cooking, if desired. Serve the fish with the remaining 1 cup barbecue sauce.

THE COWBOY WAY

A lot of folks visiting the Wildcatter come for the hiking, mountain biking, and all-terrain vehicle off-roading. There are good fossils to be found, too, as well as old arrowheads left by the Comanche who roamed here long ago. There's also a six-point sporting clays shooting range that even people who don't like hunting will enjoy. The clay pigeons come from every direction, like birds do, so it's a challenging way to learn good rifle skills.

BARBECUE SAUCE FOR FISH

MAKES 4½ CUPS

Bob makes this barbecue sauce by the gallon at the Wildcatter. You can use it on tilapia, catfish, or shrimp, too. It keeps in the refrigerator for 4 to 5 days.

4 cups of your favorite bottled sweet barbecue sauce

2 tablespoons brown sugar

2 tablespoons red wine vinegar

2 tablespoons soy sauce

2 tablespoons Worcestershire sauce

1 tablespoon minced garlic

2 chipotle chiles, finely chopped

½ cup finely chopped fresh cilantro

Combine all the ingredients in a large bowl. Working in batches, process the mixture in a blender or food processor until smooth. Store in an airtight container in the refrigerator.

BOB'S FAMOUS BABY BACK RIBS

SERVES 4

If you don't have a smoker, get one. It's the only way to make ribs taste like Bob's. Note that Bob says this rub only takes on its full flavor after it is cooked on the ribs. Trust him, he knows what he's talking about! It's best made the day before you want to use it.

2 pounds pork baby back ribs

¾ cup freshly squeezed lime juice

2 cups Bob's Famous Rib Rub (recipe follows)

Pull the silver skin off the backs of the ribs. Season the racks liberally with the fresh lime juice and the rub. Prepare a smoker for indirect heat. Cook for 2½ hours at 225° to 250°F. Remove the ribs from the heat, wrap them tightly in heavy foil, and transfer them to a warmer or an oven set at 200°F for 30 minutes before serving.

BOB'S FAMOUS RIB RUB

MAKES 3 CUPS

½ cup plus 2 tablespoons coarsely ground black pepper

1 cup dried oregano

½ cup paprika

1 tablespoon plus 1 teaspoon celery seed

½ cup plus 2 tablespoons kosher salt

1 tablespoon plus 1 teaspoon dry mustard

1½ cups brown sugar

2 teaspoons ground cinnamon

2 teaspoons minced garlic

2 teaspoons garlic powder

Mix all the ingredients together in a medium bowl. Store in an airtight container until ready to use.

PORTERHOUSE STEAKS WITH WILDCATTER STEAK RUB

SERVES 8

Here's a dinner entrée your guests will talk about for a long time after they've gone home. It doesn't get better than this. Guests at the Wildcatter almost never fail to leave without buying a few packages of Bob's rubs, which are sold in the gift shop. Once you try this, you'll see why.

1 to 1½ cups Wildcatter Steak Rub (recipe follows)

4 (1-pound) porterhouse steaks, about 1 inch thick

3 teaspoons olive oil

To prepare the steaks for grilling, place the rub on a wide plate. Rub each steak with the oil and place on top of the rub. Pat ample amounts of the rub all over each steak. Place on a grill over medium, ashy coals. Grill for 14 to 16 minutes for medium-rare (145ºF internal temperature) to medium (160ºF internal temperature), turning once. Transfer from the grill to a platter and allow the steaks to rest for 5 minutes. Remove the steak from the bones and carve into slices. Serve immediately.

WILDCATTER STEAK RUB

MAKES 2 CUPS

The beef base used in this rub is found in the same grocery store aisle as beef bouillon granules and cubes. You'll find yourself using this rub often, so you may as well double the recipe. It will keep for up to 6 months, stored in an airtight container in a cool, dark place.

⅓ cup granulated beef base

1 tablespoon kosher salt

½ cup coarsely ground black pepper

1 tablespoon cornstarch

2 tablespoons dried oregano

½ cup paprika

1 tablespoon thyme leaves

1 teaspoon onion powder

1 teaspoon ground cinnamon

1 teaspoon garlic powder

1 tablespoon minced garlic (dry)

Mix all the ingredients together in a small bowl. Rub on steaks when you're ready to grill.

WILDCATTER CREAMED SPINACH

SERVES 8

Whoa, Nelly! This is some super-rich spinach. If you think you don't like green vegetables, this will change your mind forever.

1 large yellow onion, chopped

½ cup plus 1 tablespoon unsalted butter

¼ cup all-purpose flour

1 tablespoon salt

1 cup heavy cream

½ cup chicken broth

1 teaspoon ground nutmeg

1 teaspoon cayenne pepper

1 teaspoon garlic powder

5 strips crisp bacon, chopped

4 ounces cream cheese

½ cup grated Parmesan cheese

¼ cup slivered almonds, toasted

3 pounds spinach, washed, dried, and
    coarsely chopped

In a small pan, sauté the onion in 1 tablespoon of the butter until just tender, 5 to 10 minutes. Remove from the heat and set aside. In a larger pan, melt the remaining ½ cup butter and allow it to brown slightly. Whisk in the flour over low heat, cooking until the roux is a light gold color. Add the cream, broth, nutmeg, cayenne, garlic powder, bacon, cream cheese, and Parmesan. Mix together and continue to cook over low heat until the cheese has melted. Add the sautéed onion, toasted almonds, and spinach, mixing well. Cook until thoroughly heated. Serve warm.

PATTIE'S POUND CAKE WITH BERRIES AND RASPBERRY-CHAMBORD SAUCE

SERVES 12 TO 14

This is Bob's mom's recipe for their family's favorite dessert, served at every family get-together since Bob was a little kid. You can top it with ice cream or fresh whipped cream, with or without the berries and sauce I recommend here.

1 cup unsalted butter, at room temperature

2 cups sugar

½ teaspoon baking powder

½ teaspoon baking soda

4 eggs, beaten

2 teaspoons vanilla extract

2 teaspoons almond extract

1 cup buttermilk

3 cups all-purpose flour, sifted twice

Preheat the oven to 350°F. Butter and lightly flour a Bundt pan. Cream the butter and sugar together. Add the baking powder, baking soda, eggs, and extracts. Gradually add the buttermilk and flour, alternating a little at a time. Pour into the prepared pan. Bake for about 1 hour, or until the cake is golden brown.

Serve with Raspberry-Chambord Sauce (page 18) and garnish with fresh raspberries and blackberries.

RASPBERRY-CHAMBORD SAUCE

MAKES 2 CUPS

This sauce is great on the pound cake, as well as drizzled over cheesecake or with Toby's Crème Brûlée (page 20). If you can't find fresh raspberries, use frozen ones that you've thawed and drained well.

1 cup fresh raspberries

1 cup fresh blackberries

1 cup confectioners' sugar

¼ cup Chambord

3 tablespoons freshly squeezed lemon juice

In a blender or food processor, process all the ingredients together and then strain the mixture through a fine-mesh sieve to remove the seeds. Discard the seeds. Cover and refrigerate for 1 hour. If you like a fancy presentation, drizzle the sauce from a squeeze bottle to decorate the plate.

THE COWBOY WAY

Each of the cabins at the Wildcatter Ranch is named for some kind of local lore. The Marlow is named for a local family who happened to be the inspiration for *The Sons of Katie Elder*, the John Wayne movie. It's filled with western art and images of the Marlows. Each cabin has a remote-controlled gas fireplace, so you don't even have to get out of bed to adjust the flame. A few feet away from the cabins is a swimming pool and a hot tub, good for relaxing after a day on the ranch trails.

TOBY'S CRÈME BRÛLÉE

SERVES 8

Toby Little is the assistant kitchen manager at the Wildcatter. He makes this great crème brûlée—classic, simple, and really rich!

1 cup plus ½ cup sugar

12 egg yolks

3 cups heavy cream

1½ cups whole milk

2 teaspoons vanilla extract

2 cups white chocolate chips, melted

Fresh berries, for serving

Preheat the oven to 350°F. Mix ½ cup of the sugar and the egg yolks together in a large bowl. In a saucepan, bring the cream, milk, and extract to a full boil. Remove from the heat. Pour a little cream mixture into the egg mixture and whisk well to temper it and prevent the eggs from cooking. Slowly add the remaining cream mixture to the eggs. Add the melted white chocolate. A foam will appear on the surface; skim it away before pouring into the custard cups.

Place eight 8-ounce custard cups in a long roasting pan and pour hot water into the pan until it reaches 2 inches up the sides of the custard cups. Remove the foam from the cream mixture and pour the mixture carefully into the cups until each is one-half to three-quarters full. Cover the pan tightly with plastic wrap and heavy foil. Bake for 40 minutes, or until the mixture is firm with just a tiny section at the centers still a little jiggly. Remove the cups from the pan, cover them lightly with plastic wrap, and place them in the refrigerator until chilled, at least 1 hour.

When ready to serve, divide the remaining 1 cup sugar equally among the tops of the custards. Use a chef's torch to lightly brown the tops of the brûlées, or place them under a hot broiler for just a couple of minutes, watching closely to see they do not burn. Serve with fresh berries.

WILDCATTER TOP-SHELF MARGARITA

SERVES 1

This delicious margarita is the creation of Tracy Botkin, the bartender and floor manager at the Wildcatter's Steakhouse. To rim your glass with salt, spread some kosher salt onto a small plate. Dip the top of the glass into a little water and then dip the wet rim into the salt.

2 ounces Patrón silver tequila

1 ounce Cointreau

½ cup freshly squeezed lime juice

1 to 1½ teaspoons sugar

¾ cup sweet-and-sour mix

Splash of lemon-lime soda

Lime wedge, for garnish

Pour all the ingredients in a shaker. Shake well until the sugar is dissolved. Pour into a salt-rimmed glass filled with ice, and top with the splash of lemon-lime soda. Garnish with a lime wedge.

CHUCK WAGON COWBOYS

PERINI RANCH

BUFFALO GAP, TEXAS

For anyone living in or traveling through Texas, one of life's great pleasures is eating supper at Perini Ranch Steakhouse, a place that serves up the Cowboy Way every day: As soon as you drive onto the property, you see longhorn cattle. Just walking into the ranch's comfortable restaurant, with old-brick floors and handmade wooden furniture, you're transported to another era, one where life was easier, simpler. It's a working ranch at Buffalo Gap, a little-bitty village just south in Abilene, where owner and cowboy cook Tom Perini makes the Ranch-Rubbed Prime Rib, ranch beans, and Squash and Hominy Casserole you'll find on the next pages—some of the best food I've ever tasted.

I know people who can't go more than a couple of weeks without the Sunday fried chicken dinner at Tom's place, but I'm sold on his steaks. I've been lucky enough to cook with Tom at lots of events, some of them at the ranch and some at food festivals around the state. His authentic 1890s chuck wagon, with its giant hoops, creaking sideboards, wooden wheels, and cookbox filled with vintage cans and an old clock, goes with him to food and history events all over the United States. Over the years, he's taught me plenty about historically accurate cowboy cooking, which includes a lot of stews, beans, and anything else you can cook in a Dutch oven.

. . . I LIKE TO SIT IN A ROCKING CHAIR AND OVERLOOK THE ROLLING LANDSCAPE CALLED THE CALLAHAN DIVIDE, A PLACE KNOWN FOR ITS TOWERING COTTONWOOD TREES AND LONG, LOW MESAS.

In April, Tom and his wife, Lisa, host the Buffalo Gap Wine and Food Summit, one of the most popular culinary events in Texas. Each year they have me and a handful of chefs such as West Texas native Stephan Pyles, out to cook at different functions during the event. One of the highlights is the chance to visit with Fess Parker, the actor who played Davy Crockett on TV, now a Santa Barbara, California, winemaker, who is good friends with Tom and Lisa.

All the good times at this Buffalo Gap landmark means that it's a hard place to leave, and I like killing an extra day at the restored houses on the ranch, like the 1885 farmhouse, with its long porch where I like to sit in a rocking chair and overlook the rolling landscape called the Callahan Divide, a place known for its towering cottonwood trees and long, low mesas. I'm an early riser, so I spend the first daylight watching the wild turkey and deer moving around. Nighttime is good for sitting on the deck around a fire pit, talking to Tom and Lisa about how lucky we are to live the Cowboy Way, in a world where we still get to cook on a chuck wagon and keep company with longhorn cattle.

LISA'S CAESAR SALAD

SERVES 6

This is the signature salad at Perini Ranch Steakhouse, and it's really easy to make. Use a good-quality Parmesan, like Lisa Perini does, and be sure to use sourdough bread to make your croutons so your salad is as good as Lisa's.

6 tablespoons olive oil

6 cloves garlic, minced

1 teaspoon dry mustard

1 teaspoon coarsely ground black pepper

1 teaspoon salt

3 teaspoons capers with juice

3 anchovies, chopped

2 tablespoons tarragon vinegar

2 tablespoons freshly squeezed lemon juice

1 head romaine lettuce, rinsed, drained, and torn into pieces

½ cup coarsely grated Parmesan cheese

2 cups sourdough croutons

To make the dressing, combine the olive oil, garlic, mustard, pepper, salt, capers, anchovies, vinegar, and lemon juice in a medium bowl and mix thoroughly with a fork. Toss the dressing with the lettuce in a large bowl, then sprinkle with the cheese and top with the croutons.

KING BEEF OVEN BRISKET

SERVES 10

Tom Perini usually makes his brisket in the smoker, but you'll find this a snap to make at home. Make it for Sunday supper and slice the leftovers for sandwiches to eat on Monday and Tuesday.

2 tablespoons chili powder

2 tablespoons salt

1 tablespoon garlic powder

1 tablespoon onion powder

1 tablespoon freshly ground black pepper

1 tablespoon sugar

2 teaspoons dry mustard

1 bay leaf, crushed

1 (4-pound) beef brisket, trimmed

1½ cups beef stock or broth

Preheat the oven to 350°F. To make the rub, combine the chili powder, salt, garlic powder, onion powder, pepper, sugar, mustard, and bay leaf in a small bowl, and mix thoroughly. Season the brisket on both sides with the rub. Place in a roasting pan or Dutch oven and roast uncovered for 1 hour. Add the beef stock or broth and enough water so that there's about ½ inch of liquid in the pan. Cover tightly with heavy foil (or the lid, if using a Dutch oven), decrease the oven temperature to 300°F, and continue cooking for 3 hours or until fork-tender. Slice the meat thinly across the grain. Top with the juices from the pan.

RANCH-RUBBED PRIME RIB

SERVES 10

Perini Ranch Steakhouse prime rib is known far and wide, and it's one of the reasons that Texas Monthly *magazine named Perini one of the top three steakhouses in the state. My favorite way to eat this is with a horseradish cream that you can make easily by blending a cup of sour cream with a tablespoon (or more, if you're game) of horseradish.*

½ cup kosher salt

1 cup coarsely ground black pepper

2 tablespoons all-purpose flour or cornstarch

2 tablespoons garlic powder

2 tablespoons dried oregano

1 (10-pound) boneless prime rib

Preheat the oven to 500°F. Thoroughly combine the salt, pepper, flour, garlic powder, and oregano in a small bowl, and rub the mixture over the entire surface of the meat. Place the roast on a wire rack in a roasting pan to keep it out of the drippings. Roast for 45 minutes to seal the juices, then decrease the oven temperature to 300°F and roast to the desired doneness. Use a meat thermometer to measure the internal temperature: 145°F is medium-rare and 155° to 160°F is medium. Allow the meat to rest for 10 minutes before you slice it. Serve with horseradish sauce.

AUTUMN PEAR CRISP

SERVES 6 TO 8

Tom and I baked this dessert in a Dutch oven over the coals of a campfire we built next to his chuck wagon at the ranch, but yours will be just as good in your oven. We used red pears in season; you can substitute peaches or apples or whatever looks good at the farmers' market.

6 to 8 red and green pears (about 4 cups), cored and sliced

Juice of 1 lemon

1 tablespoon ground cinnamon, divided

½ cup unsalted butter

1 cup all-purpose flour

1 cup light brown sugar

¾ cup chopped pecans (optional)

Preheat the oven to 350°F. Place the pears in the bottom of a 9 by 9-inch baking dish. Sprinkle with the lemon juice and half the cinnamon. In a mixing bowl, combine the remaining cinnamon, the butter, flour, brown sugar, and pecans. Crumble on top of the fruit and bake for 45 minutes or until it's brown and bubbly. Top with ice cream or fresh sweetened whipped cream and serve warm.

SQUASH AND HOMINY CASSEROLE

SERVES 10 TO 12

This is a signature dish at Perini Ranch Steakhouse, and it's different from side dishes you find at most steakhouses. You can make it in a big casserole dish or in individual baking dishes—it's that special.

3 pounds yellow or squash zucchini

2 large sweet onions, chopped

½ cup water

1 (20-ounce) can white hominy, rinsed and drained

2 or 3 jalapeños, seeded and finely chopped

8 to 10 ounces Monterey Jack cheese, grated

1 (8-ounce) package cream cheese, cut into small chunks

1 egg, beaten

Preheat the oven to 350°F. Rinse the squash and slice into thin rounds. Combine the squash with the onion and water in a large sauté pan and cook, uncovered, over medium heat until just tender. Remove the pan from the heat and stir in the hominy, jalapeños, cheeses, and egg, and mix well. Butter a 3-quart baking dish. Pour the mixture into the dish, and bake for about 40 minutes, or until it's bubbling and the top begins to brown.

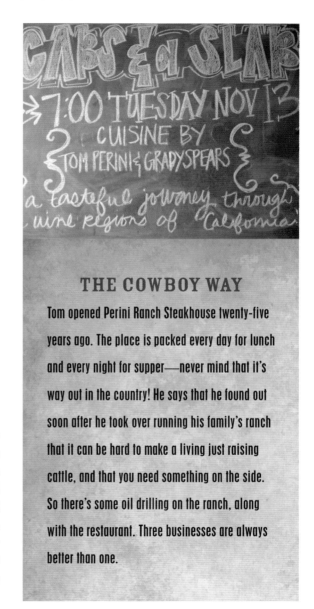

THE COWBOY WAY

Tom opened Perini Ranch Steakhouse twenty-five years ago. The place is packed every day for lunch and every night for supper—never mind that it's way out in the country! He says that he found out soon after he took over running his family's ranch that it can be hard to make a living just raising cattle, and that you need something on the side. So there's some oil drilling on the ranch, along with the restaurant. Three businesses are always better than one.

TOM PERINI'S CHUCK WAGON STEW

SERVES 20

The fat from the brisket and the bacon drippings add flavor to this hearty stew. Tom says to leave the pot on the fire for a long time to "let the flavors marry."

1 (8-pound) beef brisket, trimmed

Salt and freshly ground black pepper

¼ cup bacon drippings

3 cloves garlic, finely chopped

3 medium white onions, chopped

4 to 6 medium potatoes, peeled and cubed

1 cup corn kernels, cut from the cob

1 (28-ounce) can chopped tomatoes

1 (6-ounce) can chopped green chiles

Cut the brisket into bite-sized cubes and season with salt and pepper. In a large, heavy pot, brown the meat in the drippings and add the chopped garlic and onions. If necessary, brown the meat in batches, adding portions of the garlic and onions as you go. After the meat has browned, add enough water to cover and bring to a low boil, cooking until tender, about 1 hour. When the brisket is tender, add the remaining ingredients, and additional water if necessary, and bring back to a slow boil until the stew is fully cooked. Adjust the seasonings to taste.

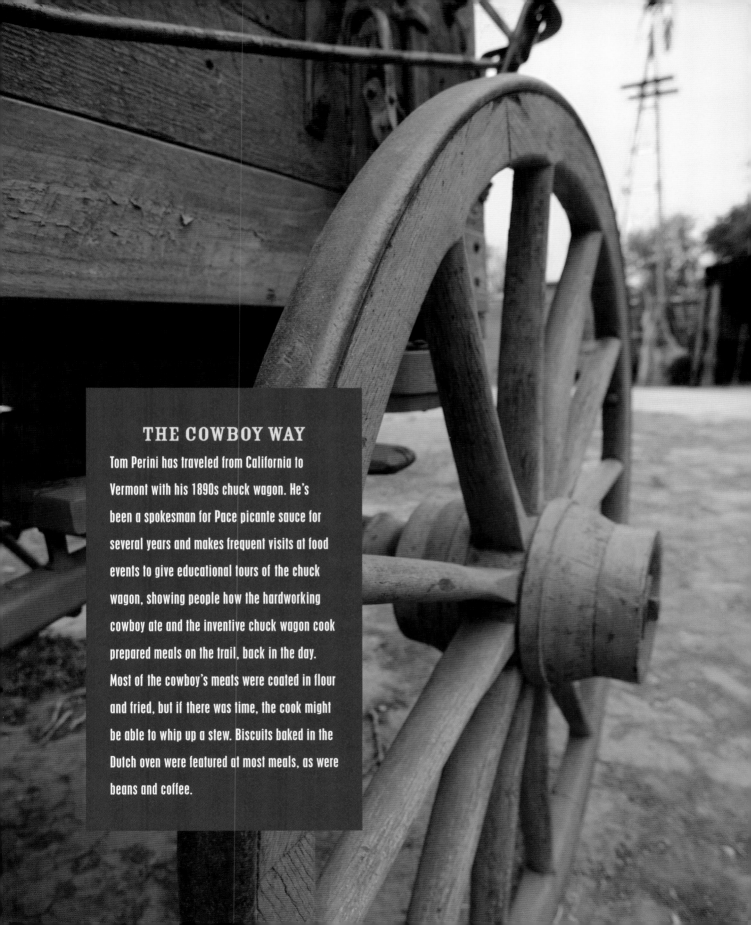

THE COWBOY WAY

Tom Perini has traveled from California to Vermont with his 1890s chuck wagon. He's been a spokesman for Pace picante sauce for several years and makes frequent visits at food events to give educational tours of the chuck wagon, showing people how the hardworking cowboy ate and the inventive chuck wagon cook prepared meals on the trail, back in the day. Most of the cowboy's meats were coated in flour and fried, but if there was time, the cook might be able to whip up a stew. Biscuits baked in the Dutch oven were featured at most meals, as were beans and coffee.

GREAT-GRANDMOTHER'S HOECAKES

SERVES 4

This southern specialty is a variation of good, ol' corn bread, and sometimes we call it hot-water corn bread. You might be tempted to deep-fry 'em, but don't. All that oil will weigh them down. Cook them like this for crisp, hot perfection.

1 cup white cornmeal

½ teaspoon salt

¾ cup boiling water

2 to 4 tablespoons bacon drippings or
    unsalted butter

Combine the cornmeal and salt in a medium bowl. Stirring constantly, add the boiling water in a slow, thin stream. Beat until the batter is smooth. Form the hoecakes by pinching off palm-sized portions and patting them out with your hands to shape them. If the batter is too hot, use a spoon. Coat a cast-iron griddle or skillet with the drippings, then place the hoecakes on griddle and fry until golden brown, 4 to 5 minutes. Flip the cakes and cook them on the other side. Have a bowl of old-fashioned molasses on hand for dipping.

TOM'S RANCH BEANS

Serves 6 to 8

In Texas, we like to soak beans overnight in water, then start cooking early in the morning and slow-cook all day. It's a great Sunday meal, with a big pan of corn bread or hoecakes on the side.

1 pound dried pinto beans

4 ounces salt pork

3 or 4 cloves garlic, minced

Kosher salt

1 tablespoon chili powder

1 jalapeño, sliced (optional)

½ cup chopped fresh cilantro (optional)

Rinse the beans and remove any stones or dirt. Cut the pork into thin strips and rinse. In a large pot, combine the beans, pork, garlic, salt, and chili powder, and cover with water. Boil over medium heat until the beans are tender, about 2 hours. The beans should always be covered with water, so add hot water as you're cooking if it's necessary. When the beans are tender, add the jalapeño and the cilantro. Allow the beans to sit for about 30 minutes to absorb these flavors before serving.

If you like, you can speed up the process by soaking the beans in water overnight. Then drain before beginning the cooking process, adding fresh water.

GRILLED SOURDOUGH WITH TEXAS ONION BUTTER

SERVES 10

One evening as Tom and I prepared to cook together for a big wine dinner at the steakhouse, I watched in amazement as several kitchen workers prepared hundreds of loaves of bread for the night's crowd. They knew from experience that the bread is that addictive.

½ cup unsalted butter, at room temperature

¼ cup chopped green onions, tops only

2 cloves garlic, minced

1 loaf sourdough bread

Blend the butter, green onion tops, and garlic, and refrigerate just long enough to set, about 30 minutes. Cut the sourdough into ½-inch-thick slices. Grill over a warm fire (or in a skillet or grill pan), then spread with the onion butter and serve.

THE COWBOY WAY

One of Tom's good friends and regular visitors is actor Robert Duvall, who has played his share of cowboys in movies. Bob, as Tom calls him, wrote the foreword to Tom's great cookbook, *Texas Cowboy Cooking*, and makes a point of eating at Tom's steakhouse whenever he can. Bob first ate at Perini Ranch Steakhouse with Clint Eastwood, when Bob starred in and Clint produced a movie called *Stars Fell on Henrietta*, which was shot nearby.

RANCHO DE LA OSA

SASABE, ARIZONA

IN THE DESERT OUTSIDE OF TUCSON, THERE'S SUCH A RICH MIX OF RAW AND RUGGED BEAUTY— LOW-SLUNG, STONY MOUNTAINS DOTTED WITH THE LONG-ARMED SAGUARO CACTUS, CREEKS HIDDEN DEEP IN LITTLE VALLEYS—THAT YOU MIGHT JUST WANT TO SADDLE UP AND RIDE FOR HOURS. IT'S SO PICTURE-PERFECT, YOU'D SWEAR THIS JUST HAD TO BE A SET FOR SOME HOLLYWOOD WESTERN, BACK IN THE DAY.

IT'S THE SETTING FOR RANCHO DE LA OSA, A PLACE WHOSE INCREDIBLE RANCH LIFE AND UNFORGETTABLE SOUTHWESTERN FOOD SPOILED ME

for future cowboy experiences in Arizona. The ranch sits right on the Mexican border next to a real small town called Sasabe, and its roots reach back to the 1700s: Built on an old Spanish land grant, the ranch's main building is one of the oldest haciendas in the nation. It overlooks a little plaza, or *zócalo*, covered by cactus and gigantic eucalyptus trees, surrounded by the lodge buildings.

Here, you can feel the spirit of Mexico in the stucco buildings, with their thick, sturdy walls, and the wide, shady porches. From the main ranch buildings, you can see the stables and the horses in their corrals, and, if you're up to watch the sunrise, you'll catch sight of the wranglers heading over to the kitchen to grab hot coffee and a bite to eat before heading out for an early trail ride. This part of the ranch heritage is special to owners Veronica and Richard Schultz, who continue the tradition of offering relaxing, romantic escapes into the southwest that began when guests first came to stay in 1921.

Veronica and Richard found a winner when they hired chef Ann Sullivan, who grew up in Waterloo, Iowa, went to culinary school at Johnson and Wales University in Rhode Island, and lives at the ranch with her cattle dog, Nina. Ann is a real wrangler in the kitchen, and together she and Veronica come up with delicious ranch menus. A great start to a day comes in the ranch's breakfast of huevos rancheros and pumpkin muffins, which fortify you for a long morning ride in the desert. At lunch, wranglers return for burgers and creamy

A GREAT START TO A DAY COMES IN THE RANCH'S BREAKFAST OF HUEVOS RANCHEROS AND PUMPKIN MUFFINS, WHICH FORTIFY YOU FOR A LONG MORNING RIDE IN THE DESERT.

green chile soup. After another afternoon of riding and roping, supper is something satisfying like chicken mole or Lamb Tenderloin with Green Olive Jam, Baked Acorn Squash with Pistachios, and Mom's Chocolate Cupcakes, which you'll find on the following pages.

If you go, take some time in the dining room to peruse the walls covered with old photographs of celebrities and politicians, like Lyndon B. Johnson and William O. Douglas. If you ask, you can probably see the rooms where John Wayne and Margaret Mitchell stayed, and the casita where William B. Clayton stayed in 1948 when he drafted the Marshall Plan at the ranch. And one of the most famous guests, of course, was Hollywood's favorite early cowboy, Tom Mix.

MOLE SAUCE FOR POULTRY

SERVES 8

This is an easy way to make what is usually a very complicated dish from deep inside Mexico. You can either make the sauce and bake pieces of poultry in it or you can bake the poultry separately, shred the meat and mix it into the sauce, and serve with hot tortillas. The Baked Acorn Squash with Pistachios (page 57) is the perfect side dish for this poultry mole.

½ **cup olive oil**

4 **cloves garlic, chopped**

½ **medium yellow onion, diced**

8 **tomatoes, quartered and seeded**

2 **poblano chiles, roasted, seeded, and chopped**

2 **cups chicken stock**

1 **cup plus** ½ **cup sliced almonds, toasted**

¼ **cup sesame seeds**

¼ **cup chopped bittersweet chocolate**

2 **tablespoons sugar**

1 **teaspoon ground cinnamon**

In a large pan, heat the olive oil and then sauté the garlic and onion, stirring occasionally, until the onion is translucent. Add the tomatoes and chiles and cook for 3 minutes, stirring occasionally. Add the chicken stock, 1 cup of the almonds, the sesame seeds, chocolate, sugar, and cinnamon. Cook for 5 minutes. Transfer to a blender and puree until smooth. Set aside in a pan to keep warm. Drizzle over chicken, turkey, or duck and garnish with the remaining ½ cup almonds.

MEXICAN CAESAR SALAD

SERVES 8

This is a super Caesar! I'd even add two to three thin slices of fresh jalapeño or serrano chile to the mayonnaise mixture you process in the blender. If you don't want to go to the trouble of frying tortillas, you can top the salad with pepitas, *or toasted pumpkin seeds. Queso fresco is a nice finish; find it at a Latin grocer.*

1 cup mayonnaise, divided

1 tablespoon chopped garlic

½ cup chopped fresh cilantro

⅓ cup finely chopped green onions,
    white part only

1 teaspoon kosher salt

2 teaspoons freshly ground black pepper

½ cup freshly squeezed lime juice

¼ cup anchovy paste

2 tablespoons Dijon mustard

2 large heads romaine lettuce

½ cup queso fresco

6 to 8 corn tortillas, cut into thin strips and
    fried until crisp

To make the dressing, combine ½ cup of the mayonnaise, the garlic, cilantro, green onions, salt, pepper, lime juice, anchovy paste, and Dijon in a blender or food processor. Blend until mixed. Whisk in the remaining ½ cup mayonnaise. Cover and refrigerate until ready to use.

To make the salad, rinse, trim, and tear the romaine lettuce into 1-inch pieces. Toss half of the dressing and the queso fresco with the lettuce. Serve on plates and top with the fried tortilla strips. Pass the extra dressing.

LAMB TENDERLOIN WITH GREEN OLIVE JAM

SERVES 4

I love lamb and had never had such a good condiment with it until I had this specialty of Ann's. It's really good with a nice bottle of full-bodied red wine, too.

1½ pounds lamb tenderloin, trimmed

5 cloves garlic, sliced

1 tablespoon dried oregano

3 tablespoons olive or grapeseed oil

GREEN OLIVE JAM

2 cups large green olives, pitted

1 clove garlic, chopped

½ cup sugar

½ cup apple juice

Pinch of ground coriander

3 tablespoons freshly squeezed lemon juice

Salt and freshly ground black pepper

To prepare the lamb, clean and divide the lamb loins into 6-ounce portions. In a large glass bowl, mix the garlic and oregano with the oil. Add the lamb and coat it with the oil mixture; cover tightly with plastic wrap and marinate overnight.

To prepare the jam, place the olives and garlic in a food processor and pulse until a paste is formed; set aside. Combine the sugar, apple juice, and coriander in a small pot and cook until syrupy. Add the olive paste and stir until incorporated and the olives have softened. Add the lemon juice. Season with salt and pepper to taste. The jam can be stored in an airtight container in the refrigerator for up to 2 weeks.

To cook, place the marinated lamb on a hot gas or charcoal grill and cook for approximately 4 minutes on each side or until medium-rare to medium, registering 145° to 160°F on an internal cooking thermometer. Let the lamb rest for about 5 minutes before cutting. Serve with the jam.

GOLDEN CORN BREAD MUFFINS

SERVES 10 TO 14

I like to sprinkle just a little bit of chili powder on top of the muffins before I bake them. Be sure to have lots of butter on hand to slather on when the muffins come hot out of the oven.

1 cup all-purpose flour

1 cup yellow cornmeal

2 tablespoons sugar (optional)

¾ teaspoon baking soda

¾ teaspoon salt

2 cups buttermilk

2 eggs, beaten

2 tablespoons unsalted butter, melted

Preheat the oven to 400°F. Grease muffin cups with corn or canola oil. Combine the flour, cornmeal, sugar, baking soda, and salt in a large bowl. In a separate bowl, mix the buttermilk and eggs. Stir the buttermilk mixture and melted butter into the cornmeal mixture until blended. Spoon the batter into the prepared tins, filling the cups about halfway to two-thirds full. Bake for about 20 minutes, or until golden on top and a toothpick inserted in the center comes out clean.

THE COWBOY WAY

If you've enjoyed *Cowboy U* on CMT and think you're made of the right stuff, you can sign up for a weeklong course at the Arizona Cowboy College. Offered at the Lorill Equestrian Center in Scottsdale, this intense camp puts you on a working cattle ranch and teaches you horsemanship, along with real cowboy skills, such as riding, roping, and horseshoeing, so that you can work with cowboys on a four-day roundup. This isn't for tenderfoots and sissies, because you'll be eating by the campfire and sleeping under the stars.

THE COWBOY WAY

Every year in March, the Festival of the West takes place in Scottsdale, Arizona. One of the big draws is the Chuck Wagon Cook Off, when competitors bring their authentically restored chuck wagons to compete in 1880s-style cattle-drive cooking. Even the utensils have to be typical of that period, with no stainless steel or plastic in sight. Dressed in costumes of the era, cooks prepare beef, biscuits and other breads, beans, potatoes, and fruit cobblers over an open wood fire.

ASPARAGUS AND PORTOBELLO ENCHILADAS IN CHIPOTLE CREAM

SERVES 10 TO 12

Man, talk about good–these enchiladas will satisfy even a meat-lover. The chipotle cream adds richness, and the sharp cheddar on top is a great finishing touch.

CHIPOTLE CREAM

3 cups sour cream

6 tablespoons buttermilk

1 teaspoon adobo sauce (from canned chipotle chiles)

ENCHILADAS

2 pounds asparagus

3 teaspoons olive oil

4 large portobello mushrooms, sliced

4 cloves garlic, finely chopped

2 chipotle chiles (from can)

8 ounces ricotta cheese

1 teaspoon ground cumin

1 cup grated Parmesan cheese

2 large eggs, lightly beaten

12 (8-inch) flour tortillas

2 cups low-sodium chicken broth

2 cups grated sharp cheddar cheese

½ cup snipped fresh cilantro, for garnish

To make the cream, blend the sour cream and buttermilk in a small bowl and let stand at room temperature for 12 hours, to thicken. After it's thickened, add the adobo sauce to the sour cream mixture and set aside at room temperature until you're ready to bake.

To make the enchiladas, preheat the oven to 325ºF. Wash the asparagus and trim the tips into 1-inch pieces, then cut another half-inch piece below the tip. (You can use the rest for soup or discard.) Heat the olive oil in a medium pan and sauté the asparagus, portobello mushrooms, and garlic over medium heat for about 2 minutes. Remove from the heat. Chop the chiles and mix with the ricotta cheese, cumin, Parmesan cheese, and eggs. Add to the sautéed vegetables.

Heat the tortillas in a lightly greased frying pan, then wrap them in aluminum foil to keep them soft. Spray two 8 by 8-inch glass baking dishes lightly with nonstick cooking spray. Fill one tortilla at a time with the asparagus mixture and roll it up. Arrange the enchiladas in the baking dishes–do not layer them. Pour 1 cup of the chicken broth into each dish. Pour 1½ cups of the chipotle cream into each dish atop the enchiladas and chicken broth. Bake the enchiladas, uncovered, for approximately 30 minutes, then sprinkle the cheddar cheese on top and bake for an extra 15 minutes, or until the cheese melts. Sprinkle the cilantro on top and serve.

BAKED ACORN SQUASH WITH PISTACHIOS

SERVES 4

This dish will please even picky eaters, including those who claim they don't like squash. The butter and maple combine to make the creamy texture even more luxurious, and the pistachios give good contrast.

½ cup pistachio nuts, unsalted, roughly chopped

2 small acorn squash

¼ cup unsalted butter, melted

2 tablespoons pure maple syrup

Preheat the oven to 450°F and toast the pistachios for 10 minutes. Set aside to cool. Decrease the oven temperature to 350°F. Slice the squash crosswise in half and trim a bit off the bottoms so the halves will sit flat. Scoop out and discard the seeds, and place the squash in a baking pan, cut side down. Cover with foil and bake for 45 minutes to 1 hour, or just until soft. In a small bowl, combine the butter and maple syrup. Remove the squash from the oven and brush the halves with the butter-maple mixture and sprinkle with the pistachios. Return the squash to the oven for 15 minutes longer. Serve hot.

THE COWBOY WAY

People who want to learn how to ride horses—or get better at it—come to Rancho de la Osa for the horseback program, which is one of the best in the West, thanks to good instruction for novices and well-mannered, well-trained horses. Wranglers take you out for a different ride of two hours or more twice a day, always going here and there in the scrubby grasslands of the high Sonoran Desert. If you really want to cowboy up, you sign on for hardworking cattle roundups and the rustic, hearty cowboy cookouts.

MOM'S CHOCOLATE CUPCAKES

SERVES 12

Wow, this takes me back to being a kid. A big glass of cold milk is the perfect side to a plate of these cupcakes.

3 ounces unsweetened chocolate, chopped

2½ cups all-purpose flour

1½ teaspoons baking soda

½ teaspoon salt

2⅓ cups light brown sugar

½ cup unsalted butter, at room temperature

1 cup sour cream

3 large eggs, beaten

1 teaspoon vanilla extract

1 cup water

Preheat the oven to 350°F and prepare 12 muffin cups for baking, using cupcake foils or papers. Melt the chocolate in a double boiler. Sift the flour, baking soda, and salt into a large mixing bowl and then add the brown sugar and mix to combine. Add the butter and the sour cream, and mix on medium speed to make a thick paste. Add the eggs, melted chocolate, and vanilla, then increase the speed to high and beat for 2 minutes. Stop and scrape down the sides of the bowl.

Resume mixing on medium-high for 5 seconds. Reduce the mixer speed to low and then slowly pour in the water. Pour the batter into the prepared muffin tins, filling the cups halfway to two-thirds full, and bake for approximately 30 minutes, or until a toothpick inserted in the center comes out clean. Frost with Sasabe Buttercream Frosting (page 62).

MOM'S YELLOW BUTTER CUPCAKES

SERVES 12

These cupcakes are dangerous, they're so good. You can use a different extract–try lemon or almond instead of the vanilla, or see what looks interesting on the shelf at the store–to get a different flavor.

3 cups all-purpose flour

1 tablespoon baking powder

¼ teaspoon salt

1 cup unsalted butter, at room temperature

2 cups sugar

4 large eggs, lightly beaten

1 cup whole milk

1 teaspoon vanilla extract

Preheat the oven to 350°F and prepare 12 muffin cups for baking, using cupcake foils or papers. Sift the flour, baking powder, and salt into a medium bowl and then set aside. Cream together the butter and sugar together at medium-high speed until the mixture is light in color. Lower the speed and gradually pour the eggs into the butter mix. Once they've been incorporated, beat the mixture on medium speed until ivory colored, 3 to 5 minutes. Decrease the mixer speed to low and then add the flour mixture alternately with the milk and vanilla. Pour the batter into the prepared pans, filling the cups about halfway to two-thirds full, and bake for approximately 25 minutes, or until a toothpick inserted in the center comes out clean. Frost with Sasabe Buttercream Frosting (page 62).

SASABE BUTTERCREAM FROSTING

MAKES 3 CUPS

Once you've made this, you may want to experiment with a different extract, like orange or maple.

1 cup unsalted butter, at room temperature

1 teaspoon vanilla extract

4 cups sifted confectioners' sugar

2 tablespoons milk

In a large bowl, cream the butter with an electric mixer. Add the vanilla. Gradually add the sugar, 1 cup at a time, beating well on medium speed. Scrape down the sides and the bottom of the bowl often. When all the sugar has been mixed in, the icing will appear dry. Add the milk and beat at medium speed until the mixture is light and fluffy. Keep the bowl covered with a damp cloth until ready to use. For best results, keep the icing bowl in the refrigerator when not in use. Refrigerated in an airtight container, this icing can be stored for 2 weeks. Rewhip before using.

For chocolate buttercream frosting, add ¾ cup cocoa powder along with the confetioners' sugar.

FRED'S TEXAS CAFÉ

FORT WORTH, TEXAS

EVERYBODY KNOWS THAT THE WEST IS FULL OF LARGER-THAN-LIFE CHARACTERS AND OTHER FOLKS WORTH TELLING STORIES ABOUT—JUST LOOK AT CALAMITY JANE AND WILD BILL HICKOK. WELL, TEXAS IS NO DIFFERENT, AND WE STILL HAVE PLENTY OF THAT WILD WEST SPIRIT RIGHT HERE IN FORT WORTH, MY HOMETOWN. IN FACT, FORT WORTH IS KNOWN FAR AND WIDE AS "THE PLACE WHERE THE WEST BEGINS," THANKS TO A NEWSPAPER PUBLISHER WHO LOVED THE TOWN'S COWBOY HERITAGE.

One who eats, drinks, and lives the Cowboy Way is Terry Chandler, the self-billed Outlaw Chef, whose life is all about cowboy cooking, both on the range with his chuck wagon and in town at his down-home café. He's a Fort Worth native who spent a lot of his childhood with a grandpa who was part Cherokee and a grandma who grew up in West Texas ranch country, folks who showed Terry the pleasures of hearty, Cowboy Way cooking. What's more, Terry's great-uncle Guy Goen was a West Texas chuck wagon cook of renown, cooking big ol' get-togethers at the family's Bar-Z Ranch on the panhandle's Caprock.

"I'VE BEEN IN TEXAS FOR SIX YEARS AND THIS IS THE BEST TIME I'VE EVER HAD!"

Back in Fort Worth, Terry grew up in his parents' little café, named Fred's for the family dog. Terry was a dishwasher there before he learned how to cook, and he was also bustin' broncs in the local rodeos. While in the Marine Corps, Terry was deployed to places all over the world, and that's how he came to love street food from many different cultures. After the corps, Terry cooked everywhere from a seafood restaurant on a North Carolina beach to a guest ranch in southern Colorado to a pizza joint in Fort Worth, before settling in to cook at Fred's Texas Café, which he eventually took over from his dad.

66

Terry's specialty is cooking global versions of Wild West dishes. The Green Chili Cream Gravy, Ranchero Grilled Quail, and other delectables found on the following pages are often specials at Fred's. Everybody loves this little joint, and it's even been featured on the Food Network's *Diners, Drive-Ins, and Dives*.

Over the years, Terry has combined some classic cooking techniques he picked up from other chefs with his chuck wagon experience. He dresses up in period costume to cook things like Eggs over Sourdough-Battered Chicken-Fried Steak with Fire-Roasted Tomatillo Hollandaise at chuck wagon events all over the country, and he brings along his posse of chuck wagon cooks to pitch in. The Outlaw Chef even had a gig recently as ranch cook during round up at one of the most important cattle ranches in state history, the legendary Four Sixes Ranch in West Texas.

Terry and I teamed up not long ago to cook a big ol' chuck wagon brunch starring dishes like Cheddar Pan de Campo and Wild Mushroom Fried Taters that you'll find in this chapter. This wasn't just any brunch; it was for the Sweethearts of the Rodeo. These women are members of the National Cowgirl Hall of Fame and Museum in Fort Worth, and several of them have ranches across North Texas. The legendary Edwards Ranch, which hosted our big brunch, is one.

Terry brought his 120-year-old Springfield chuck wagon and his crew—that's Terry "Bulldog" McLeroy, Dan Carey, Jim "Skillet" Wiginton, and Bo Powell, or the "Aught-Zero Boys"—and we whipped up food like you'd never expect at a chuck wagon! The Sweethearts all had a really good time; I even heard one of them, a woman from New York, call a friend on her cell phone and say, "I've been in Texas for six years and this is the best time I've ever had!"

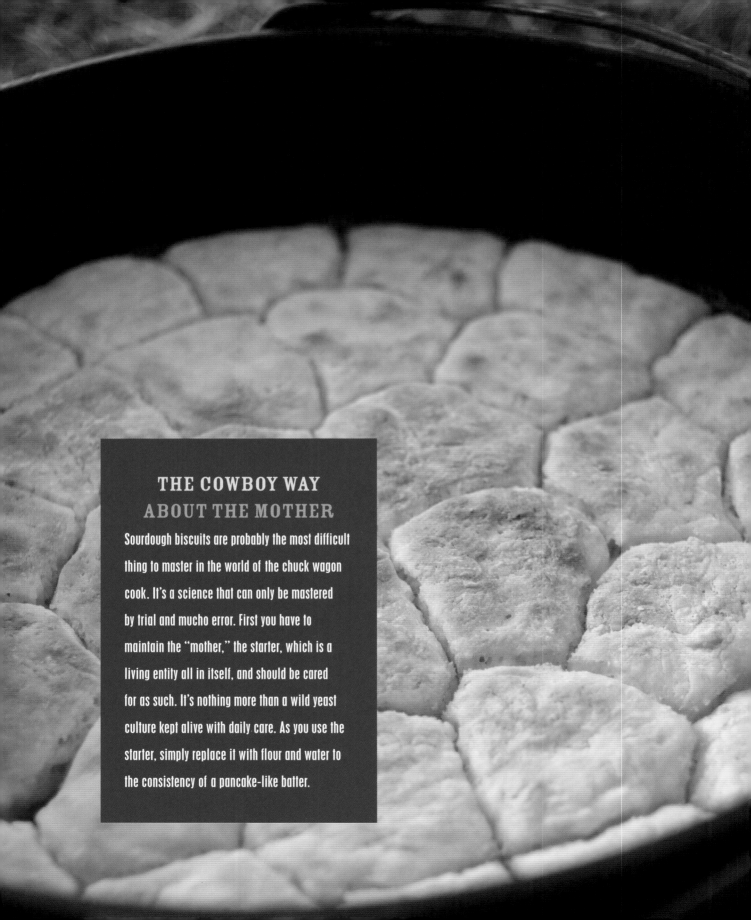

THE COWBOY WAY
ABOUT THE MOTHER

Sourdough biscuits are probably the most difficult thing to master in the world of the chuck wagon cook. It's a science that can only be mastered by trial and mucho error. First you have to maintain the "mother," the starter, which is a living entity all in itself, and should be cared for as such. It's nothing more than a wild yeast culture kept alive with daily care. As you use the starter, simply replace it with flour and water to the consistency of a pancake-like batter.

THE OUTLAW CHEF'S SOURDOUGH BISCUITS

SERVES 10 TO 12

Every cowboy cook makes sourdough biscuits according to his own special traditions. That's true especially of my buddy Terry Chandler. Note that the sourdough starter is used in several recipes and takes a couple of days to develop enough to use, and keep in mind that the sponge must be made 6 to 8 hours in advance.

STARTER

4 russet potatoes

2 cups all-purpose flour

SPONGE

1 cup whole milk

1 cup sourdough starter (see recipe above and sidebar at left)

2 cups all-purpose flour

To make the sourdough starter, peel the potatoes, put them in a large glass bowl or crock, cover them with water, and allow them to soak in a warm place for a minimum of 3 hours but preferably overnight. The wild yeast spores that float around in the air will find their way into the potato water, creating a white, foamy surface on the water; that's the yeast for your starter. Transfer 2 cups of the potato water to a separate glass bowl, jar, or crock and discard the rest. Slowly mix the 2 cups flour into the potato water, stirring well to create a batter-like consistency. Allow the starter to sit in a warm, dark place, covered with a towel or cheesecloth secured with a string, for 2 days before using. Stir it with a clean wooden spoon a few times a day. (After this initial time, you can keep your starter going by storing it in the refrigerator in a glass or plastic container with a lid in which you've made a few holes to allow gasses to escape. You'll need to "feed" the starter every few days by removing 1 cup of the starter–give it to a friend or throw it away–and replenishing the remainder by mixing in 1 cup of water and 1 cup of flour.)

To make the sponge, mix the milk, starter, and flour in a large bowl; you need to allow for the volume to double. Stir well and set aside in a warm place, covered with a towel or cloth secured with a string. Allow this to sit for 6 to 8 hours or overnight.

BISCUITS

1 cup unsalted butter, melted

3 cups all-purpose flour

1 tablespoon salt

1 tablespoon baking powder

⅓ cup sugar

4 cups sponge (page 69)

To make the biscuit dough, pour the melted butter into a large pan, at least 10 by 13 inches, or a large Dutch oven. Set aside. Whisk together in a bowl the flour, salt, baking powder, and sugar, and transfer to a large bread board, making a crater in the center large enough to pour the sponge in without it spilling over the edges. Now, add the sponge, and with a small wooden paddle, mix the dry ingredients into it, gently folding the dough. Do not overwork or knead the dough, or your biscuits will be too dense. Dust your board or work surface with a little flour. With a rolling pin, gently roll out the dough until it is about 1½ inches thick. Use a little extra flour on top to keep the dough from sticking to the rolling pin. With a biscuit cutter or a soup can, cut the biscuits from the dough, one at a time, and roll in the melted butter at the bottom of the pan or Dutch oven. The biscuits should be crowded together in the pan to create good height. When the pan is filled, set it aside in a warm, dry place to allow the biscuits to rise, at least 90 minutes. The longer they rise, the more intense sourdough flavor they'll provide. Preheat the oven to 400°F and bake the biscuits for about 20 minutes, or until golden brown. Note that humidity, ambient temperatures, barometric pressure fluctuations, and elevations all affect the outcome.

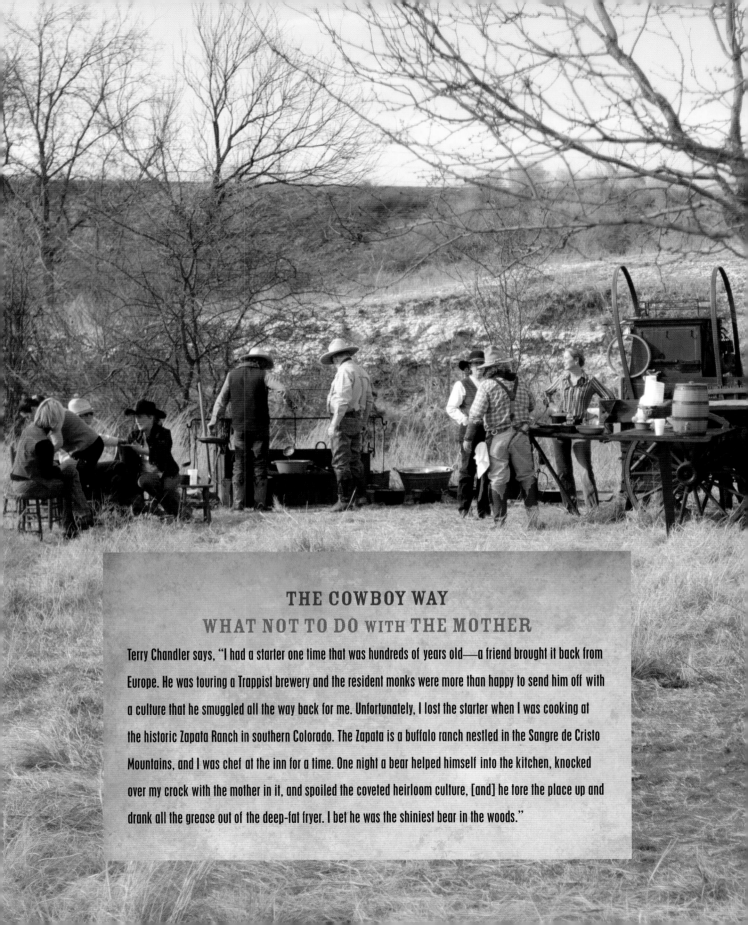

THE COWBOY WAY
WHAT NOT TO DO WITH THE MOTHER

Terry Chandler says, "I had a starter one time that was hundreds of years old—a friend brought it back from Europe. He was touring a Trappist brewery and the resident monks were more than happy to send him off with a culture that he smuggled all the way back for me. Unfortunately, I lost the starter when I was cooking at the historic Zapata Ranch in southern Colorado. The Zapata is a buffalo ranch nestled in the Sangre de Cristo Mountains, and I was chef at the inn for a time. One night a bear helped himself into the kitchen, knocked over my crock with the mother in it, and spoiled the coveted heirloom culture, [and] he tore the place up and drank all the grease out of the deep-fat fryer. I bet he was the shiniest bear in the woods."

GREEN CHILE CREAM GRAVY

SERVES 10 TO 14

In Texas, you can't eat biscuits without a good, homemade gravy made with real cream. Terry's special gravy for our Sweethearts brunch was made with fire-roasted green chiles. He likes Hatch or any other long, green chile from New Mexico, but poblano chiles will work, too.

6 large green chiles

1 pound hickory-smoked bacon

¾ cup all-purpose flour

4 cups heavy cream

½ teaspoon salt

½ teaspoon freshly ground black pepper

Roast the green chiles over an open heat source or under the broiler in an oven until they are black and blistered; transfer to a closed container to allow them to steam. Once the chiles have cooled, about 20 minutes or so, put on gloves to peel, seed, and chop them into a medium dice. Set the chiles aside. Fry the bacon in a skillet over medium heat. When the bacon is crisp, remove it and set aside to drain on paper towels; reserve the bacon for putting on top of *pan de campo*, if desired. To make a roux, stir the flour into the bacon grease over medium heat, stirring constantly until the flour stops foaming. Add the cream, increase the heat to medium-high, and stir until the gravy begins to thicken. Decrease the heat to medium or medium-low, continue to stir, and add the salt and pepper. Do not let the gravy boil. Stir in the green chiles, remove from the heat, and serve hot over biscuits.

CHEDDAR PAN DE CAMPO

SERVES 12 TO 14

This camp bread is a great appetizer. The easiest way to make it is to take some of the biscuit dough, roughly the size of your fist, and roll it out to fit in the bottom of a Dutch oven. Because it's like a pizza, you can also roll it to fit a pizza stone. Top it and bake. If you don't have the homemade dough on hand, use this recipe.

CRUST

1 cup all-purpose flour

½ teaspoon baking powder

½ teaspoon salt

½ teaspoon sugar

TOPPINGS

¾ cup grated cheddar cheese

½ cup sliced jalapeño

½ cup julienned medium red onion

To make the crust, combine the flour, baking powder, salt, and sugar in a bowl. Add just enough cold water so that you can work the mixture into a dough. On a floured work surface, roll the dough out to a ½ to ¾-inch thickness. Top with the cheese, jalapeño, and onion. If baking over a campfire in a Dutch oven, put hot coals on top of the lid and allow to bake until the cheese is melted and bread is baked, about 20 to 30 minutes. Or preheat the oven to 400°F, place the dough with the toppings on a pizza stone or a large baking sheet, and bake for 10 minutes, or until brown at the edges and bubbling at the center.

THE COWBOY WAY

Terry explains, "Extra biscuit dough can be made for flatbread, which we call *pan de campo*, or cobbler crust. My grandmother used to make cinnamon twists for us kids with the leftover dough.

Let's say I want a nice sourdough dinner roll for an evening meal. Well, I'll just make twice as many biscuits at breakfast, cooking half for the morning meal and using the leftover dough for supper. *Pan de campo*, or camp bread, is called pizza outside the cowboy world. In Greece they call it pita, in Mexico it's a tortilla, and in the Indian Nations, it's fry bread—fried instead of baked. Melted cheese on top is a nice touch, but it's certainly not necessary. I've seen *pan de campo*, without any topping at all, used as a welcome alternative to the usual biscuits."

WILD MUSHROOM FRIED TATERS

SERVES 6

Russet potatoes are the ones to use here, because new potatoes don't brown well. It's important to soak the potatoes first to make them crisp when they cook. Be sure to use a large skillet or the results will be mushy.

4 large russet potatoes, peeled, quartered, and sliced to ¼ inch thick

½ cup vegetable oil

½ teaspoon salt

½ teaspoon freshly ground black pepper

1 pint fresh mushrooms, such as shiitake or morel, sliced

Cover the potatoes in water and soak them for 30 minutes to 1 hour. Pour the oil into a large skillet and heat it until it shimmers but isn't smoking. Add the potatoes to the pan and season with the salt and pepper. Stir the potatoes if they're sticking to the pan. Cook over medium heat until browned, about 5 minutes. Add the mushrooms and continue cooking for 3 to 5 minutes, or to your liking. Drain on paper towels and serve warm.

THE COWGIRL WAY

Fort Worth is home to the celebrated national Cowgirl Museum and Hall of Fame, where honorees include a number of trick riders, ranchers, horsewomen, and other folksy types who helped shape the American West. One of the coolest things the Cowgirl Museum does is sponsor Cowgirl U, a number of classes and events each year for women who wish they'd been born in the saddle—and some who just want to learn how to giddyup. Each class or event lets cowgirl wannabes hang out with some of the Hall of Fame honorees for rodeo education workshops, basic horsemanship study, outdoors photography workshops, and trips to some of the ranches out in Big Sky Country. Yee-haw.

EGGS OVER SOURDOUGH-BATTERED CHICKEN-FRIED STEAK

WITH FIRE-ROASTED TOMATILLO HOLLANDAISE

SERVES 6

Chicken-fried steak is made several different ways, but this is how Terry cooks it on his chuck wagon. Be sure to soak the steak in the sourdough starter for at least 3 hours; the tougher the steak, the longer you should soak it, as the enzymes will tenderize the meat.

STEAKS

4 pounds beef sirloin steaks, ½ to ¾ inch thick

2 cups sourdough starter (page 69)

1 cup all-purpose flour

1 tablespoon salt

1 tablespoon freshly ground black pepper

1 tablespoon garlic powder

Vegetable oil

EGGS

½ cup vegetable oil or bacon grease

12 eggs

TOMATILLO HOLLANDAISE

6 to 8 tomatillos or green tomatoes

3 eggs plus 3 egg yolks

¾ cup unsalted butter, melted

¾ teaspoon salt

Cut the steaks into pieces about 3 by 3 inches. Place the steaks on a cutting board, cover with plastic or waxed paper, and pound gently with a mallet or the bottom of a small, heavy frying pan. Transfer the steaks to a large bowl and cover with the sourdough starter. Cover the bowl and refrigerate the steaks and starter for at least 3 hours.

In a medium bowl, whisk together the flour, salt, pepper, and garlic powder. To batter the steaks, use your left hand to take a steak from the starter, shake off the excess liquid, and place it atop the flour mixture, taking care not to put your hand in the flour. With your right hand, gently press the flour mixture into the meat; flip the steak over and repeat. (If you don't maintain a separate wet hand and dry hand, you'll be a mess in no time.) Transfer the coated steak to a platter sprinkled with a little flour. Repeat the coating process with all of the steaks. If necessary, place a sheet of waxed paper between the layers of the battered steaks on the platter.

Heat ½ inch of oil in a large, deep, heavy pan over medium-high heat until it shimmers, but isn't smoking. To fry, pinch one steak by its corner and set it carefully into the hot oil, taking care not to splatter. When the bottom is browned, use tongs to turn the steak over; cook for a total of about 5 minutes. Transfer to a platter covered with paper towels to drain. Add more oil to the pan as needed, allowing it to heat before cooking more steaks. If you don't have a helper making the eggs while you cook the steaks, keep the steaks warm in an oven set at the lowest temperature.

Heat the oil over low heat in an oversized skillet, preferably 15 to 17 inches in diameter. Crack the eggs gently into the skillet and allow to cook for about 30 seconds, or until they start to whiten a bit on the bottom. Cover the skillet with a tight-fitting lid and cook for another 30 seconds, then remove from the heat. They will finish cooking as you prepare the hollandaise. Have the steaks on the plates, ready for the eggs and hollandaise.

Roast the tomatillos over a flame or under a broiler until they are blistered and slightly burned. Force the tomatillos through a strainer into a clean skillet, and discard the skins. Place the tomatillo puree over medium heat and bring it up to a light simmer. Crack the eggs into a cold skillet and add the yolks. Whisk them well and bring the heat under the skillet up just high enough to heat them slightly but not cook them. Gradually add the eggs to the tomatillo puree, whisking until foamy. Find a kitchen helper to assist: Have your helper place 2 cooked eggs on top of each steak while you add the butter to the tomatillo puree, stirring vigorously until the mixture starts to thicken; add the salt, stir, and pour over the eggs and steak to serve.

BLUEBERRY-PEACH COBBLER

SERVES 10

This is a great dessert dish for brunch. You can bake it in a Dutch oven over the campfire, adding coals to the top of the oven's lid, or bake in your oven at home.

½ cup unsalted butter

1 cup all-purpose flour

¾ cup plus ½ cup sugar

2 teaspoons baking powder

½ cup milk

2 cups peeled, sliced peaches

2 cups fresh blueberries

Preheat the oven to 350ºF. Melt the butter in a 2½-quart baking dish. Combine the flour, ¾ cup of the sugar, the baking powder, and milk in a medium bowl. Stir well and spoon the batter carefully onto the hot butter, but do not stir. In a separate bowl, mix the remaining ½ cup sugar with the peaches and blueberries. Carefully spoon the fruit over the batter. Bake until the crust rises through the fruit and browns, 30 to 45 minutes.

RANCHERO GRILLED QUAIL
WITH VAQUEROS MIGAS

SERVES 6

This good ol' favorite is a fixture on the menu at Fred's Texas Café, and ranchero sauce is about as classic as it gets in Tex-Mex cooking philosophy. We put it on everything, from eggs to steaks, potatoes, or fish tacos. It's a rich, deep red sauce that looks good on a plate too. Be sure to get ancho chile pods that feel somewhat soft, like raisins, not paper-dry.

RANCHERO SAUCE

6 ancho chile pods

2 teaspoons vegetable oil

6 cloves garlic, chopped (not minced)

1 medium yellow onion, chopped

1 to 4 jalapeños, depending on heat desired

½ teaspoon salt

½ teaspoon brown sugar

¼ teaspoon fresh ground cumin

6 drops of freshly squeezed lime juice

QUAIL

6 whole quail, semi-boneless, if possible

2 tablespoons extra-virgin olive oil

salt and freshly ground black pepper

To make the sauce, reconstitute the chile pods in a bowl by covering them with hot water and letting them soak for 20 to 30 minutes. Discard the seeds and stems and puree in a blender to make a pulp. Set aside. In a large pan, heat the oil until medium-hot and add the garlic, onion, and jalapeños. Sauté over medium heat until the garlic has browned slightly, about 5 minutes. Add the ancho pulp. Sprinkle with salt, brown sugar, and cumin and stir. Simmer for 10 minutes. Add the lime juice and stir well. Serve warm over the quail.

To make the quail, flatten the quail as much as possible, cutting them down the backbone with a pair of shears, if necessary. Brush the quail with the olive oil, then season with salt and pepper. Prepare a gas or charcoal grill to medium-high heat and cook for 6 to 8 minutes per side, turning once. The ideal internal temperature is 145°F. Take care to use long tongs. Serve with Vaquero Migas (page 86) and top with the ranchero sauce.

If you have some native quail from a hunting trip, great. If not, you can find some at the butcher counter of fine grocery stores or in Southeast Asian markets. Or you can always order quail online; see The Cowboy's Chuck Box (page 207). As a last resort, substitute with Cornish game hens.

VAQUERO MIGAS

SERVES 6

Migas *is a Mexican version of scrambled eggs with crispy fried corn tortilla chips mixed in. There are plenty of variations, but the one hard-and-fast rule is that you can't use flour tortillas–that's not authentic! Use yellow or white corn tortillas.*

16 yellow corn tortillas

Vegetable oil

12 eggs, beaten

½ teaspoon salt

½ teaspoon freshly ground black pepper

1 cup grated cheese of choice, cheddar or a good Mexican white is preferred

¼ cup finely chopped onion

¼ cup finely chopped firm but ripe tomato

2 jalapeños, finely chopped (optional)

Cut the tortillas into rectangles about 1 by 2 inches. Heat 1½ inches of oil over medium-high heat. When the oil is hot but not smoking, fry the tortilla pieces, stirring to keep them from sticking together. Before they are crisp, transfer the chips to a platter covered with paper towels to drain. Set aside. Discard about half of the oil, return the skillet to the heat, and add the eggs to the skillet. Season with salt and pepper and stir constantly. As the eggs begin to set, add the tortilla chips and continue to stir, scraping the bottom of the pan. When the eggs reach a soft scramble, fold in the cheese, followed by the onion, tomato, and jalapeño. Serve with the grilled quail and ranchero sauce.

BLOOD ORANGE MIMOSAS

SERVES 8

Mimosas are always a terrific brunch drink, but why not get creative? Instead of regular orange juice, use the vivid juice from blood oranges, or experiment with mango puree.

1 bottle sparkling wine, such as prosecco or cava, chilled

4 cups blood orange juice

Fill 8 champagne flutes halfway with the sparkling wine and top with the blood orange juice. Serve.

BLOODY MARÍA

SERVES 8

Here's a good variation on the Bloody Mary, using tequila instead of vodka for a Mexican cowboy cocktail.

1½ cups silver tequila

6 cups tomato juice

1 tablespoon plus 2 teaspoons Worcestershire sauce

1 tablespoon Tabasco jalapeño sauce

Pinch of sea salt

Pinch of freshly ground black pepper

Juice of ¼ lime

16 super-thin slices serrano chile, for garnish

8 green onions, tops trimmed, for garnish

Combine all the ingredients except the chile and green onion in a pitcher. Stir well and strain into tall glasses filled with ice cubes. Garnish with 2 serrano slices and 1 green onion per glass. Serve.

THE COWBOY WAY

Terry Chandler says when he first visited the Bar Z Ranch in the Texas panhandle as a kid, he was impressed with how the chuck wagon suppers came together. Here's how he described it: "First, the men of the family would begin construction on a large brush arbor to create shade for the multi-day soiree, which was centered mainly on catching fish from the many stock ponds located around the ranch. After the construction of the arbor, they would dig a long, skinny ditch and build a monster fire at one end to supply the cooking ditch with hot coals, needed for Dutch oven cooking and grilling. Here, the men turned out three meals a day for the 100+ people gathered at the ranch. Then, on the final day, we would have a big fish fry with the fish we all caught."

CANADIAN COWBOYS

HOMEPLACE RANCH

CALGARY, ALBERTA

THE CELEBRATION OF CANADA'S COWBOY HERITAGE IS THE CALGARY STAMPEDE, WHICH CALLS ITSELF THE GREATEST OUTDOOR SHOW ON EARTH. IT TAKES PLACE IN ONE OF THE MOST SCENIC PLACES IN THE WEST, A REACH OF LOW PLAINS SHADOWED BY THE MAJESTIC, SNOW-TIPPED ROCKY MOUNTAINS, FOR TEN DAYS IN JULY EACH YEAR. THIS IS HOME NOT ONLY TO THE WORLD'S LARGEST OUTDOOR RODEO AND RECORD-SETTING LIVESTOCK AUCTIONS, BUT ALSO TO MY FAVORITE EVENT: THE HIGHLY ENTERTAINING CHUCK WAGON RACES.

. . . LIFE AND FOOD ARE SIMPLY BETTER ENJOYED OUTDOORS, IN A SADDLE OR BESIDE THE FIRE.

More than 1 million people attend each year's festivities, and it's become a place where I make an annual journey to cook with cowboys from up north.

Among the ranchers who make the Stampede such a memorable experience are Rob Matthews (a former Stampede president) and his wife, Marci, whose Limousin cattle make great Alberta beef. When Rob and Marci built their dream house in the mountains just north of Calgary, I cooked Molasses-Rubbed Alberta Beef Tenderloin, Buffalo Sliders with Canadian Cheeses, and Candied Bacon with Goat Cheese for the 250 people attending the house-warming party. It was just after New Year's, when there was plenty of snow on the ground and everyone was hungry for lots of my cowboy cooking.

On the same trip, my wife, Jen, and I took our son, Gage, to spend the day at a neighboring ranch a few minutes from Rob and Marci's home. Homeplace is a working ranch that brings an authentic cowboy experience to life for regular folks who need a connection with the past and a taste of down-home cowboy food, Canadian-style. There's nothing fussy here; in pretty weather, folks enjoy

a day in the saddle after a breakfast of fried eggs and Homeplace Ranch Apple Muffins, followed by an evening beside the campfire, and a steak.

Homeplace owner Mac Makenny grew up nearby and bought the ranch, now almost a century old, in the 1970s. Originally, he led horse pack trips into the wilds of nearby Kananaskis Country, but he says more folks wanted to sleep in beds than on the ground, so he converted the original ranch home to a small guest lodge and added a second small lodge. Folks usually spend time talking about the Cowboy Way with Brad McCarthy, ranch wrangler and cook, who has some really solid theories about why life and food are simply better enjoyed outdoors, in a saddle or beside the fire. I liked checking out the historic family photos, like the one of Mac's parents, taken in 1936 as they were saddling up to go get married. The artfully stitched chaps and beautifully beaded gloves they were wearing in the photo are items Mac displays in the house. Mac shares wonderful stories of his parents' adventures in those wild days, such as his mother's work as a cook on pack trips and the Indians she befriended.

BUFFALO SLIDERS WITH CANADIAN CHEESES

SERVES 12

This is one of the several handheld appetizers we made for Rob and Marci's giant housewarming party. Their guests ate these as fast as we could get them grilled and served on the platter! If you can find bison, it's really good–and lean. The Canadian cheddar is great, too.

2 pounds ground bison or chuck beef

¾ cup grated Canadian white cheddar cheese

1 medium red onion, finely chopped

2 teaspoons kosher salt

1 tablespoon coarsely ground black pepper

12 fresh biscuits or mini hamburger buns

Prepare a charcoal or gas grill to medium-high heat. In a large mixing bowl, combine the ground meat, grated cheese, onion, salt, and pepper thoroughly with your hands. Divide the mixture into 12 small patties, making sure they are compacted and firm. Place the patties on the hot grill and cook for 5 minutes on each side, or until they register an internal temperature of 160°F. Serve on biscuits or buns with your favorite condiments.

MOLASSES-RUBBED ALBERTA BEEF TENDERLOIN

SERVES 10

Alberta's beef is really good; if you can get your hands on some, you'll be glad. The rub seals in the juices while cooking. We sliced the tenderloin and served it on corn bread muffins to make hearty appetizer portions, but you can slice it into larger, entrée portions and serve it with grilled asparagus.

1 (5- to 6-pound) beef tenderloin, trimmed

1 to 2 tablespoons vegetable oil

1 cup dark brown sugar

1 cup light brown sugar

½ cup coarsely ground black pepper

¼ cup plus 2 tablespoons kosher or sea salt

Preheat the oven to 500°F and line a baking sheet with foil. Rub the tenderloin with the oil, completely covering it; set aside. In a bowl, combine the sugars with the pepper and salt. Coat the tenderloin on all sides with the seasoning mix, packing it in with your hands so that the seasoning sticks to the meat. Sear the beef in a large skillet until browned on each side, about 3 minutes per side. Transfer to the baking sheet and finish in the hot oven, roasting for 5 to 10 minutes to the desired doneness. Use a meat thermometer to make sure the tenderloin is cooked properly; an internal temperature of 145°F is medium-rare.

CANDIED BACON WITH GOAT CHEESE

SERVES 20

I came up with this appetizer for Rob and Marci's party and their guests went crazy over it. It may seem like a little bit of trouble, but I promise—it's worth it. You can save yourself some cleanup time by lining your baking sheet with parchment paper or quick-release foil.

½ cup dark brown sugar

½ cup light brown sugar

1 tablespoon coarsely ground black pepper

20 strips good-quality, thick-cut slab bacon

½ cup goat cheese, at room temperature

In a medium bowl, combine the dark and light brown sugars with the pepper, mixing until well blended. Line two cookie sheets with parchment paper or quick-release foil and spread the sugar mixture over the sheets. Press one strip of bacon at a time into the sugar mixture and then flip it over to coat the other side. Place the bacon strips side by side on the sugar as you finish, to form a single layer in the pan. Repeat with the remaining bacon on the other cookie sheet. Set aside at room temperature for 30 minutes. Preheat the oven to 400°F. Place the cookie sheets in the oven and bake for 15 to 20 minutes, or until the bacon is darkened and cooked through. Remove the sheets from the oven and let cool for 5 to 7 minutes. Once the bacon has cooled and hardened, cut the strips in half and top each with a dollop of goat cheese. Serve.

BRAD'S SHEPHERD'S PIE

SERVES 6

This easy recipe is a favorite supper at Homeplace Ranch. Brad McCarthy makes it with whatever variety of vegetables he has on hand, and serves a bowl of extra vegetables on the side. You can't go wrong with brown gravy on top.

2 teaspoons vegetable oil

1 pound ground sirloin

1 medium yellow onion, diced

3 cloves garlic, minced

1 cup green or yellow beans, trimmed and cut into 1-inch lengths

2 cups peeled, sliced carrots

3 ears corn, shucked, with kernels removed

Kosher salt and freshly ground black pepper

3 teaspoons dried thyme

3 teaspoons dried rosemary

3 cups mashed potatoes

Preheat the oven to 350°F. Heat the vegetable oil in a large skillet over medium heat and add the meat and onion. Cook until the meat browns and the onion is translucent, about 5 minutes. Add the garlic, green beans, carrots, and corn; cover and cook, stirring occasionally, until the vegetables are just tender, 5 to 7 minutes. Season with the salt and pepper and herbs, and stir. Remove from the heat and scoop the mixture into a 6 by 9-inch buttered casserole dish. Cover with the mashed potatoes and bake until browned at the edges, about 30 minutes. Serve with brown gravy, if desired.

JEN'S BUTTERMILK-BLUEBERRY LEMON SQUARES

SERVES 16

Jen is definitely the baker in our family, and this is one of her specialties. She and Marci made several pans of these for the party, and there weren't any left over.

Crusts for 2 (9-inch) pies

1½ cups dried blueberries

2 cups sugar

2 tablespoons cornmeal

5 eggs, beaten

⅔ cup buttermilk

½ cup unsalted butter, melted

Juice of 2 lemons

2 teaspoons lemon zest

1 tablespoon vanilla extract

1 teaspoon ground nutmeg

Preheat the oven to 375°F. Sprinkle a long rimmed baking sheet (at least 10 by 13 inches) with flour. Spread the pie crusts over the bottom and sides of the sheet, cutting to fit your pan as necessary. Sprinkle the dried blueberries on the crust. In a medium bowl, combine the sugar and cornmeal. Add the eggs and buttermilk and mix well. Stir in the butter, lemon juice and zest, vanilla, and nutmeg. Pour the buttermilk mixture over the berries. Bake for about 30 minutes, or until set and just browning on top. Allow to cool for 15 to 20 minutes before serving.

THE COWBOY WAY

When he's not working the ranch horses and leading trail rides, Brad rustles up family-style meals at the main house. In a kitchen dating from 1920—showcasing an iron stove that was part of the original 1912 homestead, as are several of the outbuildings scattered around the property—he turns out a ranch hands' breakfast of fried eggs, smoked sausage, pancakes, pastries, and more. Brad's back in the kitchen each evening to prepare things like shepherd's pie. On Saturday night, there's a big steak barbecue at the pit outside, where poplar wood adds good smoke flavor to the Alberta beef. On Sunday, there's a traditional turkey dinner with all the trimmings.

RANCH POTATO PANCAKES

SERVES 6

Brad makes ranch potatoes–hash browns baked with bacon, sour cream, cheddar, and green onions–to go with steak dinners. He and I used the leftover potatoes to make these pancakes for a good brunch dish. You can serve them with salsa or top them with grated cheese.

½ cup unsalted butter, melted

1 medium yellow onion, diced

1 pound potatoes, peeled and coarsely grated

1 cup sour cream

1½ cups grated sharp cheddar cheese

½ cup chopped green onions, green and
    white parts

Kosher salt and freshly ground black pepper

1 cup chopped cooked bacon

½ cup all-purpose flour

¼ cup vegetable oil

In a large bowl, combine the butter, onion, potatoes, sour cream, cheese, green onions, and bacon. Combine the flour, salt, and pepper in a shallow dish. Shape a handful of the potato mixture into a patty and dredge in the seasoned flour. Transfer to a dry cookie sheet. Heat the oil in a large skillet over medium-high heat until it shimmers. Fry a few pancakes at a time in the hot oil until browned, turning once. Drain on paper towels and serve them warm.

HOMEPLACE RANCH APPLE MUFFINS

MAKES 12 MUFFINS

Brad makes muffins and cookies just about every day at Homeplace Ranch, and guests can help themselves to sweets and coffee any time they like. We made these muffins with fresh apples for breakfast; try Golden or Red Delicious apples in yours. You can serve these with Maple Butter (page 107), too.

1 egg

1 cup milk

¼ cup vegetable oil

2 cups all-purpose flour

¼ cup sugar

3 teaspoons baking powder

½ teaspoon sea salt

3 teaspoons ground cinnamon

2½ medium apples, cored, peeled, and coarsely grated

Preheat the oven to 350°F. Butter twelve regular (⅓-cup) muffin cups and set aside. Combine the egg, milk, and oil in a medium bowl by hand with a spoon or fork. In a large bowl, combine the flour, sugar, baking powder, salt, and cinnamon with a fork. Make a well in the center of the dry ingredients and pour the wet ingredients into it, add the grated apples, and then mix just until all the ingredients are moistened. Spoon the batter equally among the prepared muffin cups. Bake for 15 to 20 minutes, or until a toothpick inserted in the center of a muffin comes out clean.

For blueberry muffins, substitute 1 cup of blueberries for the apples. For cranberry muffins, substitute 1 cup cranberries and the zest of 2 oranges for the apples, and substitute ½ cup orange juice for half of the milk.

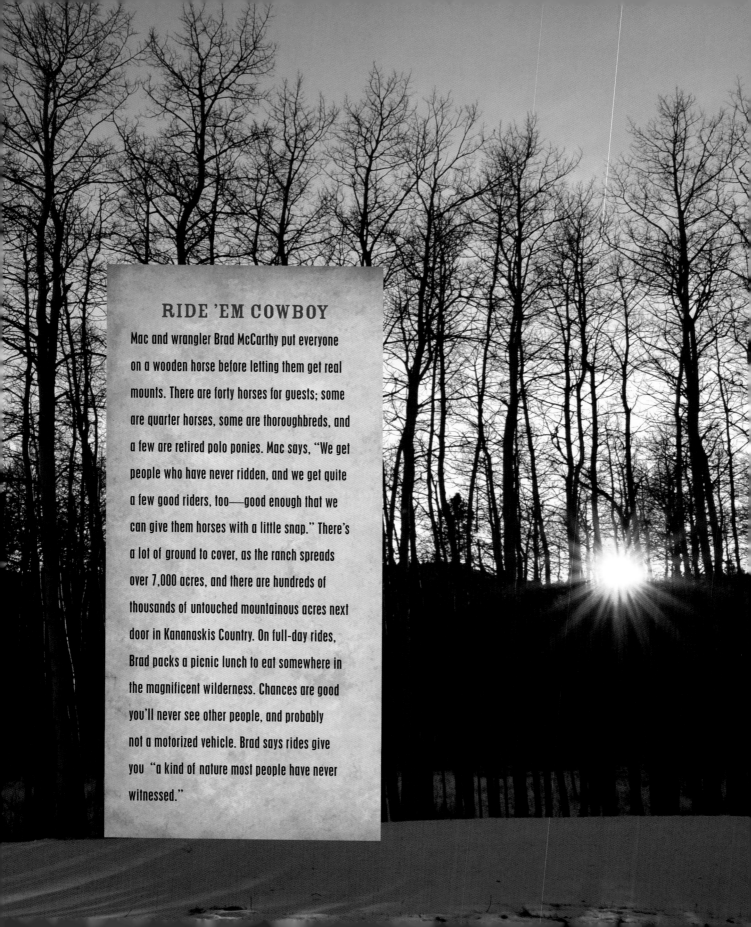

RIDE 'EM COWBOY

Mac and wrangler Brad McCarthy put everyone on a wooden horse before letting them get real mounts. There are forty horses for guests; some are quarter horses, some are thoroughbreds, and a few are retired polo ponies. Mac says, "We get people who have never ridden, and we get quite a few good riders, too—good enough that we can give them horses with a little snap." There's a lot of ground to cover, as the ranch spreads over 7,000 acres, and there are hundreds of thousands of untouched mountainous acres next door in Kananaskis Country. On full-day rides, Brad packs a picnic lunch to eat somewhere in the magnificent wilderness. Chances are good you'll never see other people, and probably not a motorized vehicle. Brad says rides give you "a kind of nature most people have never witnessed."

SKILLET BUTTERMILK CORN BREAD WITH MAPLE BUTTER

SERVES 10

This is just a great, easy dish to serve with everything from steaks and pot roast to fried chicken. If you're making it for a party, use tins for baking mini muffins.

CORN BREAD

1 cup yellow cornmeal

1 cup all-purpose flour

¼ cup sugar

1 tablespoon baking powder

¼ teaspoon salt

1 cup buttermilk

1 large egg

5 tablespoons unsalted butter, melted, cooled slightly

1 cup grated cheddar cheese

1 (10-ounce) can diced tomatoes and green chiles, drained

MAPLE BUTTER

¾ cup unsalted butter, at room temperature

3½ tablespoons pure maple syrup

To make the corn bread, preheat the oven to 400°F. Butter a cast-iron skillet. Sift the cornmeal, flour, sugar, baking powder, and salt into a medium bowl. Whisk the buttermilk and egg in another medium bowl, and then whisk in the melted butter. Add the buttermilk mixture to the dry ingredients; stir just until incorporated (do not overmix), then fold in the cheese and the diced vegetables. Pour the batter into the prepared skillet and bake for 20 to 25 minutes, or until a toothpick inserted in the center comes out clean. Serve with the maple butter.

To make the maple butter, beat the butter in a medium bowl with an electric mixer until creamy. Gradually beat in the maple syrup until well blended and smooth. Cover and refrigerate until set, 30 to 45 minutes. This can be made up to 1 week ahead and stored in an airtight container in the refrigerator.

MARCI'S SAVORY PARMESAN CHEESECAKE

Serves 20 to 30

Marci is famous for her cheesecake appetizer, which is great party food for a big crowd. You could even vary the cheeses, using blue cheese or feta, if you like. If you can find a Canadian cheddar (look online if necessary; see The Cowboy's Chuck Box, page 207), use it! Note that this is a large, dense cheesecake that you serve with an appetizer knife for spreading onto bread or crackers—not in slices like a typical cheesecake.

¼ cup wheat cracker crumbs

¼ cup grated Parmesan cheese

1 tablespoon unsalted butter, melted

4 (8-ounce) packages cream cheese, at room temperature

½ cup whipping cream

4 eggs

5 cups grated Parmigiano-Reggiano cheese

1 cup grated Canadian white cheddar cheese

½ cup shredded Gruyère cheese

⅓ cup snipped fresh chives

¼ teaspoon cracked white peppercorns

Stir together the cracker crumbs and the Parmesan. Generously butter a 9-inch springform pan with half of the melted butter. Sprinkle about 3 tablespoons of the crumb mixture into the pan, lightly dusting sides and bottom of the pan. Stir the remaining butter into the remaining crumb mixture; set aside.

Preheat the oven to 300°F. Beat the cream cheese and whipping cream in a large mixing bowl with an electric mixer on medium speed just until smooth. Add the eggs one at a time, beating until just combined. Stir the cheeses, chives, and peppercorns in with a rubber spatula until smooth. Pour the mixture into the springform pan, spreading evenly. Sprinkle the remaining crumb mixture over the top. Place the pan on a cookie sheet, and bake for 1 hour and 45 minutes. Allow to cool in the pan on a wire rack for 15 minutes. Run a knife around the inside of the pan to loosen the crust, and allow to cool for 30 minutes longer. The center may dip once it cools. When cool, spring the side of the pan and remove. Transfer to a serving platter. Serve with appetizer knives and bread or crackers for spreading.

CAESAR COCKTAIL

SERVES 6

This is the Canadian version of a Bloody Mary. According to cocktail lore, it was created by a Calgary bartender, Walter Chell, in 1969 to be the signature drink at a place called Marco's.

9 ounces vodka

6 cups Clamato juice

3 dashes of Tabasco sauce

3 dashes of Worcestershire sauce

Juice of ½ lime

6 celery spears, for garnish

Celery salt, for garnish

In a pitcher, mix the vodka, Clamato, Tabasco and Worcestershire sauces, and lime juice until blended. Adjust the seasonings to taste. Pour over ice into tall glasses, and garnish each with a celery stick and a pinch of celery salt.

THE COWBOY WAY

Homeplace Ranch is one of dozens of stops on the Cowboy Trail, which is a link through a corridor of communities in Alberta's Rocky Mountains foothills. This stretch of the West features towns and settlements established by Alberta's pioneer ranch families in the 1880s, and it's a great place to drive now to experience the history and culture of Alberta's ranching heritage. One of the best places to explore is the Bar U Ranch National Historic Site of Canada, about 1½ hours southwest of Calgary. Over the years, famous visitors there have included King Edward VIII of England and one of my favorite artists, Charles Russell. You can see exhibits on ranching culture and history here, and you can eat buffalo burgers and sourdough biscuits at the Bar U Café on site. In the Bar U's Pekisko Creek General Store, you can buy preserves, woodwork, handmade candles and soaps, and other local crafts that are true to Alberta's Old West heritage.

A TEXAS TAILGATE PARTY

ARLINGTON, TEXAS

When you're in Texas and talk turns to cowboys, it may take you a second to figure out if people mean the kind that ride horses and work with cattle or the kind that win Super Bowls and make up America's Team. And then we're talking about another kind of Cowboy Way—and I do mean the pride and joy of most Texans who love football—that's also near and dear to my heart.

Growing up in the Lone Star State, I am all about the 'Boys with the blue stars on their helmets. Like most red-blooded Texans, we live and die by the Sunday gridiron contest, and are as bitterly disappointed if they don't win as a spur-wearing cowboy is when he doesn't make the buzzer when riding a bronc in the rodeo.

Where I live, you aren't doing the Cowboy Way right on Sunday if you're not cooking up a tailgate party at a Cowboys game. To me, food gatherings at athletic events like these aren't too different from cowboys kicking back together over a beer and burger from the rodeo concession stand. And when you think about it, sipping a cold one and cooking with friends around the grill just outside the stadium is a whole lot like the cattle-driving cowboys who shared stories over coffee and steaks around the campfire, with the herd nearby.

Tailgate gatherings at Dallas Cowboys games, which take place nowadays at the new, billion-dollar Cowboys Stadium in Arlington, Texas, start some several hours before kickoff. That means we'd better have a whole lot of good food and drink for our friends who show up for the fun and festivities. We've found that our Easy South Texas Fajitas, Chicken and Roasted

Green Chile Sandwich, and Frito Pie—all of which you'll find in this chapter—
are the perfect tailgate food. And our fellow football fans who happen to be
vegetarians sure like our Portobello Mushroom Burger, too!

LIKE MOST RED-BLOODED TEXANS, WE LIVE AND

DIE BY THE SUNDAY GRIDIRON CONTEST . . .

Whether you're tailgating or cooking for your posse on your backyard grill
before watching the game on TV, you'll want some of these crowd-pleasing recipes in your saddle pack. On the following pages, you'll also find Chile con Queso
with Vegetable Escabeche, a spicy mix of pickled vegetables; Gridiron Guacamole
and Red River Salsa; and great sandwich condiments, like Chipotle Mayo, which
is the signature touch on our Blue Cheese and Bacon Burger. You can wash it all
down with a West Texas Sunrise, which you should make by the pitcher.

DUTCH'S CHICKEN AND ROASTED GREEN CHILE SANDWICH

SERVES 4

If you think grilled chicken sandwiches are boring, you haven't tried this one! The roasted green chile and the Monterey Jack cheese turn this into an addictive meal. Be sure to use organic chicken if you can; it really makes a big difference in the taste.

4 (6-ounce) boneless, skinless chicken breasts

2 tablespoons olive oil

Kosher salt

Freshly ground black pepper

2 poblano chiles, roasted, seeded, and cut in half lengthwise

4 slices Monterey Jack cheese

½ cup mayonnaise

4 hamburger buns

4 leaves green leaf lettuce

Prepare a gas or charcoal grill or heat a skillet to medium-high, and preheat an oven to 400°F. Coat each breast with the olive oil. Season each chicken breast with kosher salt and black pepper and cook on the grill or in the skillet over medium-high heat for 5 to 6 minutes on each side (you may have to cook them two at a time if you're using a skillet). Remove the chicken breasts from the heat and place them on a baking sheet. Top each breast with one roasted chile half and a slice of the cheese. Bake the breasts for 5 to 6 minutes, or until the cheese has melted. Remove from the oven and let rest. Spread the mayonnaise on both halves of each bun, lightly covering the whole piece. Place the chicken breasts on the prepared buns with the lettuce and serve warm.

DUTCH'S PORTOBELLO MUSHROOM BURGER WITH HERBED MAYO AND GREENS

SERVES 4

This vegetarian burger alternative has been a surprise hit at the Fort Worth restaurant I opened with Lou Lambert called Dutch's. Even meat-lovers go crazy for this sandwich, which is so good and hearty that you don't miss the meat. The herbed mayo really adds to the overall flavor.

½ cup olive oil

¼ cup balsamic vinegar

1 tablespoon Dijon mustard

4 portobello mushrooms, cleaned, and
    stems removed

HERBED MAYONNAISE

½ cup mayonnaise

2 teaspoons minced fresh rosemary

1 roasted garlic clove, minced

Kosher salt

4 hamburger buns, toasted

2 cups field greens, or 1 large bunch of arugula

8 thin slices tomato

4 thin slices red onion

4 slices Swiss cheese

In a large bowl whisk together the oil, vinegar, and mustard. Place the mushrooms in the marinade and let sit for at least 1 hour. While the mushrooms are marinating, make the herbed mayo, combining all the ingredients in a bowl; cover and refrigerate.

Preheat the oven to 400°F or prepare a gas or charcoal grill to medium-high heat. Remove the marinated mushrooms from the liquid and season with kosher salt. Discard the marinade. On the grill, cook the mushrooms over medium-high heat for 4 to 5 minutes on each side; in the oven, roast them, top side down, for 15 to 20 minutes, or until the mushrooms are soft. Remove from the heat and set aside.

Spread the herbed mayonnaise evenly on each half of the buns. Place each mushroom on a bottom bun and put a quarter of the greens atop each warm mushroom. Top with 2 slices tomato and a slice each of onion and cheese. Serve warm.

DUTCH'S BLUE CHEESE AND BACON BURGER WITH CHIPOTLE MAYO

SERVES 4

Nothing beats the flavor combination of blue cheese, bacon, and chipotle. You get sweet, smoky, tangy, and a little bit of fire, all in one bite. This is a great burger any way you cook it, but if you use ground sirloin, you'll taste the difference.

BURGERS

4 (8- to 10-ounce) ground sirloin or hamburger patties

Kosher salt

½ cup Chipotle Mayo (recipe follows)

4 hamburger buns

12 strips thick-sliced bacon, cooked

1 roma tomato, sliced

1 small red onion, sliced thin

¼ cup crumbled blue cheese

Prepare a gas or charcoal grill or heat a skillet to medium-high heat. Season each burger with kosher salt and cook for 4 to 5 minutes on each side. Remove the burger from the heat and let rest for 3 minutes. Spread a thin layer of chipotle mayo on the top and bottom of each bun. Place a burger on the bottom bun, then layer the bacon, tomato, and onion on top, and finish with the blue cheese crumbles. Put the top bun in place and serve warm.

CHIPOTLE MAYO

MAKES ½ CUP

½ cup mayonnaise

1 teaspoon adobo sauce from canned chipotle chiles

½ teaspoon freshly squeezed lime juice

Kosher salt

In a bowl, combine the ingredients, mixing well. Season with the salt and refrigerate, covered, until needed.

DUTCH'S CHILE CON QUESO WITH VEGETABLE ESCABECHE

SERVES 8 TO 10

This is the old-school queso recipe that mothers would throw together for the neighborhood kids back in the 1970s, and it's a staple today at Dutch's. The simplest way to put this together is in a slow cooker, such as a Crock-Pot. You can also prepare it in a heavy saucepan over the stove, as we do at the restaurant. Poblanos or New Mexican green chiles are best for this recipe.

1 tablespoon unsalted butter

½ cup finely diced red or yellow onion

½ cup finely diced tomato

½ cup finely diced roasted green chiles

¼ cup milk

16 ounces Velveeta or other easy-melt cheese, cut into 2-inch cubes

2 cups grated Monterey Jack cheese

Salt and white pepper

4 green onions, green and white parts, finely diced, for garnish

1 tablespoon coarsely chopped fresh cilantro, for garnish

Corn tortilla chips, warmed

In a large saucepan, melt the butter over medium-high heat until it begins to bubble. Add the onion and cook until it begins to become translucent, about 4 minutes. Add the tomato and roasted chiles and cook for another 4 minutes. Add the milk to the pan and then stir in the Velveeta. Decrease the temperature to low and stir the cheese mixture until it is melted and creamy, about 5 minutes. Stir in the Monterey Jack and season with salt and pepper. When the cheese has melted, about 2 minutes, garnish with the green onions and cilantro and serve with warm tortilla chips and a side of Escabeche (recipe follows). If you'd like, you can keep this warm for a party in a slow cooker.

ESCABECHE

MAKES 1 CUP

Escabeche, a Mexican-style pickled vegetable condiment, adds a whole extra dimension to cheese dip. Serve it on the side for guests to add to the queso as desired.

½ medium white or yellow onion, chopped

3 cloves garlic, minced

2 medium carrots, peeled and sliced ¼ inch thick

½ cup vinegar

1 cup water

2 teaspoons sea salt or kosher salt

2 teaspoons sugar

3 pickled jalapeños, chopped

In a saucepan, combine the onion, garlic, and carrots with the vinegar, water, salt, and sugar. Cook over medium-high heat until the vegetables are tender, 10 to 15 minutes. Drain the cooking liquid. Add the jalapeños to the onion mixture. Allow to cool, then cover and refrigerate. Use as a condiment with steak, chicken, or fish, or mix with queso for dipping.

THE COWBOY WAY

What should you be sure to take to your tailgate party, besides a wagonload of great food? You definitely ought to have some kind of canopy, which you can find anyplace that sells camping gear. It's hot and sunny at daytime football games, so you want to provide shade for your guests, even if old-time cowboys out on the range didn't have such luxuries. Of course, you need a great portable grill that can accommodate plenty of food. Be sure to bring a long table or several card tables, because you need enough room to set out plates, napkins, utensils, condiments, cups—and food! Bring tablecloths to dress up that table a little. Even if you have a tailgate on your truck, you'll still need ample seating for your guests, so pack all the chairs you can. Don't forget the cooler full of beverages, some music, and a football to throw around.

DUTCH'S FRITO PIE

SERVES 4

Frito pie is a big deal in Texas—you can find it served at plenty of concession stands at Friday night high school football games across the state. It's a traditional dish that I love to make for game-watching parties, and it's easy to serve at a tailgate party. Just put all the ingredients out on the table and let your guests build their own! You can find Cotija cheese, queso fresco, and Mexican oregano at a Latino grocery store or order them online (see The Cowboy's Chuck Box, page 207).

1 (16-ounce) bag corn chips

2 cups Dutch's Chili (page 122)

1 large red onion, diced

2 tablespoons diced jalapeños

1 cup sour cream

1 cup crumbled Cotija cheese or queso fresco

4 sprigs of cilantro, for garnish

To assemble, divide the corn chips among four bowls, mounding them into a pile in the center of each. Top each mound of chips with an even portion of the chili. Top each bowl with the onion, jalapeños, and a dollop of sour cream. Divide the cotija cheese evenly among the bowls, garnish with a sprig of cilantro, and serve warm.

DUTCH'S CHILI

SERVES 6

4 tablespoons vegetable oil

1 medium yellow onion, chopped

2 tablespoons roasted garlic

2 pounds coarsely ground beef

1 cup Red Chile Sauce (page 123)

1 tablespoon chili powder

1 tablespoon Mexican oregano

1 teaspoon ground cumin

2 medium tomatoes, diced

2 cups chicken stock

1 (12-ounce) bottle amber beer

2 teaspoons kosher salt

Heat the oil in a stew pot or Dutch oven over medium-high heat. Add the onion and garlic, and sauté until the onion is soft. Add the meat and cook until it starts to brown, stirring occasionally. Add the Red Chile Sauce, chili powder, oregano, cumin, and tomatoes, stirring well to combine. Cook for 5 to 7 minutes, then stir in the stock and beer. Lower the heat to a simmer and cook, uncovered, for 45 minutes to an hour, stirring occasionally to keep the chili from sticking. Season with the salt and remove from the heat. Serve warm.

THE COWBOY WAY

What kind of cowboy food works best for your favorite football team? Here are some ideas, based on geographic areas and the foods made famous in each.

Cincinnati Bengals: Chili

Tennessee Titans: Brisket

Buffalo Bills: Beef stew

Kansas City Chiefs: Ribs

Cleveland Browns: Sausage

Arizona Cardinals: Beans

Denver Broncos: Steaks

St. Louis Rams: Pizza

Carolina Panthers: Pulled pork

Dallas Cowboys: Burgers

RED CHILE SAUCE

MAKES 4 TO 5 CUPS,
DEPENDING ON THE SIZE OF THE ANCHOS

Ancho chiles are hot, so if you have sensitive skin, put on a pair of gloves before you cut them.

16 dried ancho chile peppers (8 ounces)

½ large white onion, peeled and diced

5 cloves garlic

6 cups water

3 medium tomatoes, diced

½ cup honey

2 tablespoons ground cumin

Kosher salt

Rinse the chiles to remove any dust or dirt. Slit each one with a sharp knife and remove and discard the seeds and stems. If you aren't wearing gloves, be sure to wash your hands very well after this. Place the peppers, onion, and garlic in a large saucepan and cover with water by 1 inch–it should be about 6 cups of water. Bring to a boil over high heat, then lower the heat and simmer for about 15 minutes. The peppers should have softened and absorbed some of the liquid. Remove the pan from the heat and set it aside without draining. Let it stand for 30 to 40 minutes.

Drain the chiles, reserving the liquid, and place the solids in the container of a blender. Strain the reserved ancho liquid through a fine-mesh sieve. Add about 2 cups of the ancho liquid to the blender. Cover and start blending at low speed, increasing to high speed as the puree takes shape. Add the toma-

toes, honey, cumin, and salt, and blend until smooth. The result will be a thick, dark red sauce. Adjust the seasonings with salt and more honey, if desired–the honey offsets the heat of the peppers. The sauce can be refrigerated, covered, for up to a week.

THE COWBOY WAY

If you really want to impress your crowd, you'll want some of the deluxe toys made for tailgating fiends. One is a portable microwave that hooks up to electricity provided by your car battery. And how about a gas-powered blender for margaritas? Those fancy rolling coolers are really nice, too. Portable grills come in every size and shape, of course; you just have to decide whether you'd rather cook over charcoal or use gas. Either way, remember to soak some wood chips ahead of time to add more smoke flavor to the food. Nowadays, the big tailgaters are bringing flat-screen TVs to watch all the pre-game action while eating and drinking, but we think good food, cooked over an open fire, is all you need.

EASY SOUTH TEXAS FAJITAS

SERVES 8

Fajitas were invented in Texas, probably on the ranch lands down south, also called La Frontera. The skirt steak is one of the most affordable cuts of beef, and it's cut thin for quick cooking. The chile marinade gives the steak a deep flavor that goes great with salsa and guacamole.

2 pounds skirt steak, sliced thin

2 cups Red Chile Sauce (page 123)

2 medium yellow onions, cut into thick slices

1 tablespoon vegetable oil

12 to 16 corn or flour tortillas

Red River Salsa (page 126)

Gridion Guacamole (page 128)

Lime wedges, for garnish

Place the steak and Red Chile Sauce into plastic container or self-closing plastic bag and marinate for 6 hours or overnight.

Prepare a gas or charcoal grill to medium-high heat or heat a skillet over medium-high heat. Toss the onion slices in a bowl with the oil to coat well, being careful not to separate into rings. Remove the beef from the sauce and discard the marinade. Grill the steak and onion slices over the fire or in a large (at least 15-inch) hot skillet, about 3 minutes per side, turning once. Warm the tortillas over the fire, too, away from direct heat, being careful not to burn them. Serve the beef and onions on a platter, with the tortillas on the side. Serve with salsa, guacamole, and lime wedges.

RED RIVER SALSA

SERVES 8

Everyone's got a favorite salsa, and I bet you're going to like this one a lot. The smoky flavor comes from roasting tomatoes, red bell pepper, and poblano chiles. Make some extra to serve on eggs and grits the morning after your big tailgate bash!

4 ripe tomatoes

1 red bell pepper

2 poblano chiles

1 head garlic, roasted

1 medium yellow onion, chopped

1 or 2 jalapeños, seeded and chopped

2 to 3 teaspoons cumin seeds, toasted

½ cup fresh cilantro, chopped

Juice of 2 limes

Kosher salt

Over a gas or charcoal grill, char the tomatoes, bell pepper, and poblanos. Transfer to a bowl, cover with a dish towel, and allow to cool. When the vegetables are cool enough to handle, put on rubber gloves and remove and discard the charred skins. Add the pulps to the working bowl of a food processor. Squeeze the roasted garlic head, removing the soft meats from their skins. Add the roasted garlic to the charred vegetables in the food processor, along with the onion, jalapeño, cumin seeds, cilantro, and lime juice. Pulse until the mixture is nubby in texture. Add salt, and serve warm or chilled. The salsa will keep in the refrigerator, covered, for 3 to 4 days.

GRIDIRON GUACAMOLE

SERVES 8

Don't use the prefab stuff—you can taste the preservatives! A good avocado, such as Hass, is essential for the best guacamole. You can play with the amount of garlic, jalapeño, and citrus to get your flavors just right. Avocados don't keep, so you'll need to eat the whole batch at once. To scoop out an avocado, cut it in half lengthwise and remove the pit. Score the avocado flesh into large squares, then use a spoon to scoop out the flesh into your bowl. It's easy.

3 to 4 ripe Hass avocados

2 ripe Roma tomatoes, chopped fine

½ cup finely chopped green onions, both
green and white parts

1 jalapeño, seeded and minced

2 cloves garlic, minced

Juice of 1 lemon or lime

¼ cup minced fresh cilantro

Kosher salt and freshly ground black pepper
(optional)

Mash the avocados in a large bowl. Add the tomatoes, green onions, jalapeño, garlic, juice, and cilantro. Mix well. Add salt and pepper, and add more juice, if you like.

WEST TEXAS SUNRISE

SERVES 4

This is a sparkly, tart cocktail that was just perfect at our last tailgate, and it went great with fajitas, burgers, and chili. You get a double-dose of citrus with lemon-flavored vodka and Paula's Texas Lemon, a very potent citrus liqueur from Austin, but you can use any lemon liqueur you can find. There's a rosy tinge from the pomegranate juice, to boot. Toss in fresh mint from your garden.

6 ounces lemon-infused vodka (such as Absolut citron)

2 ounces lemon liqueur (such as Paula's Texas Lemon)

14 to 16 ounces sparkling water (lemon-flavored is good)

1 to 2 tablespoons pomegranate juice

4 lemon wedges, for garnish

4 mint leaves, for garnish

Combine the vodka, liqueur, sparkling water, and pomegranate juice in a pitcher. Stir and pour over ice cubes in glasses. Garnish each glass with a lemon wedge and mint leaf and serve.

TROPICAL COWBOYS

BELLAMY BROTHERS RANCH

DARBY, FLORIDA

NOT EVERYONE REALIZES THAT THERE IS A RICH COWBOY CULTURE IN FLORIDA. TO EXPERIENCE IT FIRSTHAND, I VISITED COUNTRY MUSIC STARS THE BELLAMY BROTHERS AT THEIR FAMILY RANCH JUST A SHORT DRIVE INLAND FROM TAMPA. HERE, MARSHES AND SWAMPS EDGE THE COASTAL PRAIRIES, AND THE BALMY BREEZES BLOWING IN FROM THE GULF STIR THE AIR IN THE CITRUS GROVES THAT LINE THE ROADSIDES AND THE BELLAMY RANCH PROPERTY.

I had a lot to learn about the tropical Cowboy Way from Howard and David Bellamy, who grew up riding horses and helping with the family cattle business and who to this day still live in cowboy hats and boots. As we explored their ranch together, they explained that Florida's 500-year-old cattle industry helps drive the state economy, and that the state's total breeding herd is worth nearly $850 million. On top of that, Florida has about 4 million acres of pastureland and 1 million acres of grazed woodland.

THE LAND HERE IS RICH AND GREEN, AND BLOOMING CAMELLIAS SURROUND THE OLD HOMESTEAD.

The ranch was founded in 1870 by the brothers' great-grandfather, Abraham Bellamy, who made his way from South Carolina to Florida. The family has lived at the ranch ever since. Howard and David grew up singing with their late dad, Homer, playing at picnics and high school and church events, taking their cowboy music all over this part of Florida. Except for the five years they lived the high life in Los Angeles in the 1970s, they've lived right there on this ranch.

The land here is rich and green, and blooming camellias surround the old homestead. Purebred Charlois cattle and quarter horses roam around a countryside thick with fruit trees and those cool, 400-year-old oaks with branches covered in Spanish moss. During my time there, we made some of David and Howard's favorite family dishes, like Howard's Ambrosia, using some of the great fresh Florida-grown fruit, and David's Roasted Oysters with Tropical Pico, as well as Cayenne Rib-Eyes and Blackened Grouper with Orange Remoulade, all while listening to cowboy music and trading stories about ranch life.

HOWARD'S AMBROSIA

SERVES 10 TO 12

Here's a great chance to use all kinds of fresh fruit. This is an especially healthy recipe, as you sweeten it with Howard's favorite all-natural sweetener, Stevia, found at Whole Foods and other health food stores. You can adjust the quantity to suit your taste, of course.

THE COWBOY WAY

Florida's old-time cowboys had a unique way of herding cattle. They used 10- to 12-foot-long whips made of braided leather. Snapping these whips in the air made a loud "crack." That sound brought stray cattle back into line fast, and earned cowboys the nickname of "crackers." Many rode rugged, rather small horses known as "cracker ponies." Cracker cowboys also counted on herd dogs to move cattle along the trail. Their tough dogs could help get a cow out of a marsh or work a hundred steers into a tidy group. For those rough riders of Florida's first ranges, a good dog, a horse, and whip were all the tools a true cracker needed.

—from "Exploring Florida: A Social Studies Resource for Students and Teachers," College of Education, University of South Florida

2 medium to large navel oranges, sectioned

2 Fuji or Gala apples, cored and sliced

1 Granny Smith apple, cored and sliced

2 cups green or red grapes

3 kiwis, peeled and sliced

1 pint strawberries, hulled and sliced

2 bananas, peeled and sliced

1½ cups walnuts, lightly toasted

½ cup grated fresh coconut meat

3 tablespoons freshly squeezed lemon juice

8 to 10 drops Stevia

Toss all the ingredients together in a large bowl, cover with plastic wrap, and refrigerate for 20 minutes. Serve slightly cool.

ROASTED OYSTERS WITH TROPICAL PICO

SERVES 8

David loves to fire up the grill and pile on the oysters. They cook up pretty fast, so you can serve them as appetizers while your steaks are grilling for the main course.

2 mangos, peeled and diced

½ large red onion, diced

2 or 3 serrano chiles, thinly sliced

¼ cup snipped fresh cilantro

Juice of 2 limes

48 oysters in their shells, scrubbed clean

Tabasco sauce, for serving

While you bring a charcoal or gas grill up to high heat, combine the mangos, onion, chiles, cilantro, and lime juice for the pico in a bowl; toss to combine, then set aside. When the grill is hot, place the oysters in a single layer on the grate, preferably with the more rounded, deeper shells toward the fire. Roast for 5 to 10 minutes, removing with long tongs the moment each oyster pops open. After 10 minutes, discard any oysters that haven't opened. Immediately serve the oysters in their shells with the pico and with Tabasco or your favorite hot sauce.

THE COWBOY WAY

Ponce de León discovered the giant, green expanses known as Florida in 1513, and returned from Spain again in 1521, bringing along horses and Andalusian cattle, said to be the ancestors of Texas Longhorns. Thus was born the first cattle-raising space in America. The St. Augustine missionaries raised their beef in spite of conflicts with Indians and problems with insects, snakes, and terrible storms. By 1700, cattle-ranching was prevalent along the St. Johns River and in what's now the Florida panhandle, and the Seminoles ran large herds by the 1800s.

CUBAN PICODILLO

SERVES 6

The Cuban cuisine influence is found not just in Miami but throughout Florida. This meat dish is a favorite of the Bellamy family, and you'll see why with just one bite. It's comfort food, for sure, and really easy to make.

3 teaspoons vegetable oil

1½ pounds lean ground beef or turkey

1 large white onion, chopped

2 or 3 cloves garlic, chopped

1 red bell pepper, chopped

1 (6-ounce) can tomato sauce

¼ cup dry white wine

1 cup pimiento-stuffed olives, coarsely chopped

1 cup golden raisins

Kosher salt and freshly ground black pepper

3 cups fluffy cooked white rice

In a large skillet over medium heat, warm the oil and brown the meat with the onion, garlic, and pepper. Decrease the heat to medium-low and add the tomato sauce and wine. Simmer for 15 minutes. Add the olives and raisins. Add the seasonings, and simmer for 20 to 30 minutes longer. The consistency should be similar to chili. Serve hot, over the rice.

If juicy, ripe tomatoes are available, use fresh peeled, seeded, and pureed tomatoes in place of canned tomato sauce.

THE COWBOY WAY
CRACKER COWBOYS OF FLORIDA

One can thresh the straw of history until he is well worn out, and also is running some risk of wearing others out who may have to listen. So I will waive the telling of who the first cowboy was, even if I knew; but the last one who has come under my observation lives down in Florida, and the way it happened was this:

I was sitting in a "sto' do" (store door) as the "Crackers" say, waiting for the clerk to load some "number eights" (lumber), when my friend said, "Look at the cowboys!" This immediately caught my interest. With me cowboys are what gems and porcelains are to some others.

–by Frederic Remington
An excerpt from Harper's Magazine, *August 1895*

GREEN AND CITRUS SALAD WITH LEMON-BASIL VINAIGRETTE

SERVES 8 TO 10

Yep, we couldn't resist using more citrus because there's just so much good stuff to choose from in Florida. Here, we included a pomelo, which looks a lot like a grapefruit but has bright greenish-yellow skin. Inside, the very pale pink fruit is sort of spicy-sweet and tart.

SALAD

3 cups baby field greens

1 grapefruit, sectioned

2 oranges, sectioned

1 pomelo, sectioned

1 Hass avocado, peeled and sliced

1 cup walnuts, lightly toasted

¾ cup diced Spanish chorizo

DRESSING

½ cup extra-virgin olive oil

2 tablespoons plus 2 teaspoons freshly squeezed lemon juice

1 clove garlic, minced

½ teaspoon sea salt

1 teaspoon freshly ground black pepper

2 tablespoons chopped fresh basil

Place the greens in a large serving bowl and top with the fruit, avocado, walnuts, and chorizo. To make the dressing, whisk together all the ingredients. Drizzle over the salad, toss, and serve.

CAYENNE RIB-EYES WITH COOK'S LIME BUTTER

SERVES 4

Florida is cattle country, after all, and all the Bellamys love steak as much as I do. We grilled a bunch of rib-eyes and topped them with the cook's tart butter and put the platter in the middle of the dinner table, alongside the salads, for everyone to share.

LIME BUTTER

½ cup unsalted butter, at room temperature

Juice and zest of 1 lime

3 teaspoons minced fresh cilantro

RUB

3 teaspoons cayenne pepper

1 tablespoon kosher salt

3 teaspoons raw sugar

4 bone-in rib-eye steaks (about 10 to 12 ounces each)

2 to 3 teaspoons vegetable oil

Prepare a gas or charcoal grill to medium-high heat. To make the butter, combine all the ingredients thoroughly in a small bowl. Place the mixture on a sheet of waxed paper and roll tightly into a cylinder about the diameter of a half-dollar. Put it into the refrigerator or freezer to firm up—but don't freeze it solid!

To make the rub, combine the seasonings in a small bowl. Wipe the steaks dry and rub them with the vegetable oil, then pat the rub on both sides of the steak. Grill over medium-hot coals to the desired temperature, or about 145°F for medium-rare. Allow the steaks to rest for 5 minutes, then slice a thick disk of lime butter on top of each one and serve.

BLACKENED GROUPER WITH ORANGE REMOULADE

SERVES 6

There's so much fresh fish to choose from at every market in Florida, it makes even a high-plains cowboy wish he lived close to the ocean. We used grouper, a popular local gulf fish, but this recipe is perfect for snapper, mahi-mahi, and catfish, too. There's a lot of flavor and it cooks quickly—what's not to like?

ORANGE REMOULADE

½ cup olive oil

½ cup chopped green onions

½ cup spicy brown mustard

¼ cup white wine vinegar

2 cloves garlic, minced

3 teaspoons paprika

3 tablespoons freshly squeezed orange juice

3 dashes of Tabasco or your favorite hot sauce

1 teaspoon sea salt

Zest of 1 orange, chopped, for garnish

FISH

2 teaspoons dried thyme

1 to 2 teaspoons ground cayenne

1 to 2 teaspoons paprika

1 to 2 teaspoons kosher or sea salt

1 teaspoon garlic powder

1 to 2 teaspoons white pepper

½ cup unsalted butter, at room temperature

3 pounds grouper fillets

To prepare the remoulade, combine all the ingredients except the orange zest in a blender or food processor, processing until smooth. Refrigerate for 20 to 30 minutes, covered, until ready to serve. Present in a bowl, garnished with orange zest. This makes a great condiment to use on rice, too.

To prepare the fish, combine the thyme, cayenne, paprika, salt, garlic powder, and white pepper in a small bowl. Mix and set aside. Wipe the grouper fillets clean, then coat both sides of the fillets with half the butter. Pat both sides thoroughly with the spice rub. Heat a large cast-iron skillet until it is smoking hot. Add some of the remaining butter, decrease the heat to medium-high, and add the grouper fillets. Cook until nicely browned, about 3 minutes, then turn to cook the other side, adding the rest of the butter to the skillet. Cook until browned on the second side, about 2 minutes longer. Serve hot with the remoulade sauce.

PLANTAIN NACHOS WITH CREAMY BLACK BEANS

SERVES 8 TO 10

Another favorite Cuban dish found in most parts of Florida, this is a great snack to serve with mojitos or ice-cold beer. Plantains are available in most specialty markets. You can slice the plantains diagonally or into round discs. You may want to serve some of your favorite salsa alongside, too.

4 plantains

1 cup vegetable oil

1½ cups black beans, rinsed and drained

¼ cup chicken or vegetable stock

Juice of ½ lime

1 teaspoon Kosher salt

2 cloves garlic, minced

1 cup crumbled queso fresco

Peel the plantains and slice into rounds about ¼ inch thick. Heat the oil in a skillet until it shimmers. Fry the plantains until golden brown, about 2 minutes per side, removing to paper towels to drain. When all the discs are fried, repeat the process to make the rounds crispy. Drain again on fresh paper towels.

In a food processor, combine the black beans, stock, lime juice, salt, and garlic. Process until smooth. Spread on the plantain chips and scatter the queso fresco on top, or serve, topped with the cheese, as a dip alongside the chips.

MINTY MOJITOS

SERVES 4

Here's a favorite cocktail in Florida, now found in almost every bar in the nation. This recipe is one we think actually came from Havana. Go ahead and make an extra batch, because everyone loves these.

16 fresh mint leaves

1 cup freshly squeezed lime juice

4 teaspoons confectioners' sugar

Crushed ice

1 cup white rum

1 cup club soda

4 sprigs of mint, for garnish

Place the mint leaves in a small pitcher with the lime juice. Add the confectioners' sugar, then muddle the mint leaves to release the oils. If you don't have a muddler, you can gently crush the leaves with the back of a spoon. Add crushed ice and the rum, stirring well. Pour the mixture equally into 4 Collins (or other tall) glasses, and top with a splash of soda. Garnish with mint sprigs and serve.

SYLVIA'S KUMQUAT REFRIGERATOR PIE

MAKES 3 CUPS

This recipe evolved from sour orange pie, a good dish way back when sour oranges grew wild over much of Florida. Howard and David's cousin is Sylvia Young, who won first prize for this at the Kumquat Festival, which is held every winter in Dade City, Florida.

CRUST

¼ cup sour cream

½ cup unsalted butter

1⅓ cups all-purpose flour

FILLING

1 cup heavy cream

3 tablespoons sugar

⅓ cup pureed kumquat rinds

1 (14-ounce) can condensed milk

¼ cup freshly squeezed lemon juice

2 tablespoons freshly squeezed lime juice

2 tablespoons freshly squeezed orange juice

1 (8-ounce) package cream cheese,
   at room temperature

Preheat the oven to 350°F. Stir the sour cream and butter together in a bowl, then mix in the flour. (Don't overmix or the texture will be tough.) Form a dough ball and refrigerate for just a few minutes. Lightly flour a work surface, and roll the dough into a medium-thick crust. Place the pie crust dough in a 9-inch pie plate and prick the bottom of the crust with a fork. Bake the crust for about 20 minutes, or until just golden brown. Remove from the oven to cool.

With an electric mixer, beat the cream and sugar until the mixture is light, fluffy, and holds its shape when the beaters are removed. Add the kumquat rinds, condensed milk, juices, and cream cheese, beating until well combined and thickened. Scoop the mixture into the cooled pie shell and refrigerate, lightly covered with foil or plastic, until set, 2 to 3 hours.

Kumquat rinds are sweet, while the kumquat flesh is very sour. You can use the whole kumquat, if you like.

LONESOME PINE RANCH

BELLVILLE, TEXAS

Just about an hour west of Houston in the forested countryside that rolls across lush, green horse farms almost all the way to Austin, there's a place called the Lonesome Pine Ranch, a working ranch where daily life is all about raising registered Texas longhorn cattle, training quarter horses for work in cutting calves from the cattle herd, and giving visitors a chance to see buffalo up close.

It's the Cowboy Way here. Ranch owners John and Taunia Elick live on the adjacent Prairie Place Ranch, John's family ranch for more than half a century. They've raised their three daughters—Laramy, Lacey, and Ashlyn—here, near the town of Bellville, where John and Taunia are practicing attorneys.

. . . JOHN TEACHES YOU TO RIDE A HORSE PROPERLY, AND WHEN YOU'RE READY, HE TAKES YOU OUT TO WORK CATTLE WITH HIM.

The lawyer business pays the bills, but John and Taunia's hearts are in their ranch world. They come by their passion honestly: John rode saddle broncs on the rodeo circuit in Texas, Oklahoma, Arkansas, and Louisiana in earlier years, and Taunia did her rodeo bit as a barrel racer. They've even performed together at convention shows for dignitaries like Queen Beatrice of the Netherlands and a vice-premier of China.

What I like even better about the Elicks is this: In taking over the Lonesome Pine Ranch in 1989 and other nearby ranch property, they began working on preserving wildlife habitats and Texas history to share with folks from around the world, to show them what the Cowboy Way means in their part of Texas. When you come stay here, John teaches you to ride a horse properly, and when you're ready, he takes you out to work cattle with him. When you're tired, you'll rest up in one of the six historic homes that Taunia has brought to the ranch from around Austin County and restored to their original beauty. Set across about 1,600 acres covered with native pecan trees and roamed by the buffalo and longhorn herds, her vintage homes are real showplaces.

The Elicks call the collective experience Texas Ranch Life, and it's completed with the good ranch cooking they shared with me. In this chapter, you'll learn how to make John's Ancho Strip Steaks that go so well with Taunia's Corn Casserole, along with the Lonesome Pine Longhorn Chili. There are good Fish Tacos to make with the bass you'll catch in one of the ranch's lakes, and they're best eaten with Taunia's Salsa. For dessert, there's nothing better than Brazos Berry Cream Pie, and in the morning, you'll want the famous Czech pastry from this part of Texas, Mama Elick's Kolaches.

MAMA ELICK'S KOLACHES

MAKES 2 DOZEN

John Elick's grandmother brought this recipe with her from Czechoslovakia, and her great-granddaughter Ashlyn Elick used it to win one of the popular kolache contests near their ranch. You'll definitely want these for breakfast and maybe even for dessert, too. Be sure to make the Posypka topping to sprinkle on after baking.

1 cup warm milk, divided

⅓ cup sugar, divided

1 (¼-ounce) package active dry yeast

3½ cups all-purpose flour

1 egg, beaten

⅓ cup unsalted butter, melted

1 teaspoon salt

3 teaspoons vegetable oil

POSYPKA

½ cup all-purpose flour

½ cup sugar

¼ cup unsalted butter, at room temperature

⅔ cup unsalted butter, melted

In a measuring cup, stir together ⅓ cup of the warm milk (preferably 115° to 120°F) and 1 teaspoon of the sugar. Add the yeast and stir until dissolved. Let the mixture stand and become bubbly, about 10 minutes. Place the flour in the bowl of a heavy-duty mixer and make a well in the center. Add the yeast mixture, the remaining ⅔ cup of warm milk, the remaining sugar, the egg, the melted butter, and the salt at once. Mix well with the paddle attachment. Transfer the dough to a lightly floured surface and knead until smooth. Form the dough into a ball. Smooth the oil on the dough and place the dough in a clean bowl; cover with a dish towel and allow it to rise until double its original size, about 1 hour.

Line two baking sheets with parchment paper. Tear away portions of the dough (just smaller than an egg), form the dough with your hands into shapes as square as possible, and place on the baking sheets, about 2 inches apart. Cover with dish towels and allow to rise again until doubled, about 30 minutes. Preheat the oven to 350°F. Before the Kolaches go into the oven, use a small spoon or your thumb to push an indention in the center of each; fill the depression with about 2 teaspoons of your preferred filling (page 153). Bake for 18 to 20 minutes, until just golden around the tops and sides.

While the Kolaches bake, make the Posypka. In a bowl, combine the flour and sugar. Mix in the butter with a fork until texture is evenly crumbled. When the kolaches are still hot from the oven, brush with the melted ⅔ cup butter and sprinkle with the Posypka. Allow to cool before serving.

THE COWBOY WAY

You can find several communities in Central Texas that were settled in the early to middle 1800s by immigrants from Germany, Poland, and Czechoslovakia. One of the gifts from the Czechs was their delicious pastry called a kolache, a square, yeasty roll with a slightly sweet flavor and moist texture. Kolaches may be stuffed with fruit, sweetened cream cheese, or even smoked sausage. These are so popular that you can find kolache festivals and kolache-baking contests all over the place. It's not unusual to find the kolache used as a wedding pastry, instead of a cake.

THE COWBOY WAY

About 130 miles southwest of the Elicks' ranch—which isn't that far, by Texas standards—is the town of Goliad, widely known to be the place where Texas cattle ranching began. There you'll find the ruins of Mission Espiritu Santo, where according to a count in 1777, 40,000 head of longhorn cattle were being raised by the Franciscan order and area Indians, noted by the Texas State Historical Association.

KOLACHE FILLINGS

If you ask ten people in Texas their favorite kolache flavor, you'll get at least ten different answers. The Elick family is the same. John's favorite is pineapple, Taunia's is cheese, and cherry is the favorite of their daughters, Laramy, Lacey, and Ashlyn. Taunia says that she makes all the fillings ahead of time so everyone can get their choice; these keep in the refrigerator for up to 10 days.

PINEAPPLE FILLING

½ cup sugar

¼ cup all-purpose flour

1 (20-ounce) can crushed pineapple, undrained

1 tablespoon unsalted butter

In a saucepan mix together the sugar and flour and add the pineapple. Stir over low heat until thickened. Add the butter and stir until incorporated. Cool before use.

MAKES 2 CUPS

CHEESE FILLING

½ cup sugar

1 tablespoon all-purpose flour

1 cup small-curd cottage cheese

2 egg yolks

1 tablespoon unsalted butter

Combine the sugar and flour in a saucepan. Add the cottage cheese, egg yolks, and butter. Stir over low heat until thickened. Cool before use.

You can add ½ cup semisweet chocolate chips to the warm cheese mixture, stirring until smooth. Or you can top the cheese-filled kolaches with a few fresh raspberries, blackberries, or blueberries before baking.

MAKES 1½ CUPS

CHERRY FILLING

¾ cup sugar

¼ cup all-purpose flour

2 (20-ounce) cans pie cherries packed in water, drained

1 tablespoon unsalted butter

Combine the sugar and flour in a saucepan. Add the cherries and cook over low heat, stirring until thickened. Add the butter and stir until incorporated. Cool before use.

MAKES 2 CUPS

TAUNIA'S SALSA

MAKES 4 CUPS

Here's an easy salsa that goes with everything from tacos and Brunch Casserole (page 165) to chili and steaks. Taunia has to double or triple the recipe on weekends when they have lots of guests at the ranch.

2 large poblano chiles, roasted, peeled, and chopped

1 (4-ounce) can of sliced black olives, drained

1 cup chopped green onions

6 to 8 Roma tomatoes chopped

2 large avocados, chopped

1 bunch of cilantro, chopped

Juice of 1 lime

Pinch of garlic salt

Dash of Worcestershire sauce

1 teaspoon cayenne pepper

1 teaspoon freshly ground black pepper

Combine all the ingredients in a large bowl and allow to sit, covered and unrefrigerated, for about 1 hour. The salsa can be stored, covered, in the refrigerator for 2 days.

JOHN'S ANCHO STRIP STEAKS

SERVES 4

Like every rancher I've ever met, John loves to grill a big steak for supper. We had some ancho chiles–those are dried poblanos–on hand, so we added them to the steak rub we concocted together. I think they add a great smoky flavor.

**4 New York strip steaks
(about 10 ounces each)**

3 to 4 teaspoons vegetable oil

1 ancho chile, stemmed and seeded

1 cup brown sugar

½ cup kosher salt

Prepare a charcoal, gas, or wood-burning grill to medium-high heat.

Wipe the steaks dry with a paper towel, then rub with the vegetable oil. Place the ancho chile in a food processor and pulse until it's shredded as finely as it can be. Combine the ground chile with the brown sugar and salt in a bowl to create the rub and, using your hands, coat the steaks. Over medium-hot, ash-covered coals, grill the steaks to desired doneness, 11 to 13 minutes for medium-rare (that's an internal temperature of 145°F). Turn once during cooking.

FISH TACOS

SERVES 6

I spent an afternoon fishing at one of Lonesome Pine's ponds and caught a few bass. After I filleted the fish, John and I battered and cooked them in a cast-iron skillet over the ranch grill and made these tacos. You can use any kind of good frying fish.

1½ pounds bass, catfish, or tilapia fillets

¼ cup milk

¼ cup spicy brown mustard

1 teaspoon paprika

1 teaspoon cayenne pepper

½ teaspoon kosher salt

¼ cup all-purpose flour

¾ cup yellow cornmeal

1 cup vegetable oil

12 corn tortillas

Taunia's Salsa (page 156), for serving

Grated cheese, for serving

Freshly squeezed lime juice, for serving

Wipe the fish fillets dry with paper towels. Pour the milk into a wide, shallow bowl and mix in the mustard. Combine the seasonings with the flour and cornmeal on a large plate.

Heat the oil in a large skillet until smoking hot. Dip the fish fillets in the milk mixture and then dredge them in the dry mixture; use one hand for dipping the fish into the wet mixture and the other for dipping into the dry mixture so that your hands don't become gloppy. Fry in batches until golden brown on both sides, 2 to 3 minutes total. Transfer to a plate lined with paper towels to drain. While the fish is cooking, warm the tortillas in a dry skillet or on a grill. Keep the tortillas in a basket lined with warm tea towels. To serve, break the fish into pieces, piling into the tortillas with Taunia's Salsa and grated cheese. Drizzle with lime juice.

LONESOME PINE LONGHORN CHILI

SERVES 8

John and Taunia raise longhorn cattle on their ranch, and these critters yield a good lean meat, just like the buffalo they raise do. Either meat is good for making a hearty chili like this.

5 to 8 dried New Mexico red chile pods

5 to 8 cloves garlic

2 cups simmering water

1 tablespoon vegetable oil

1 large yellow onion, chopped

2 pounds coarsely ground longhorn beef

1 (28-ounce) can crushed tomatoes

2 tablespoons paprika

1½ tablespoons ground cumin

1½ tablespoons dried Mexican oregano

Kosher salt

Stem and seed the chile pods. Place the pods and garlic in a heat-proof glass bowl with the simmering (not boiling) water. Cover the bowl and set it aside for about 30 minutes. Meanwhile, heat the oil in a Dutch oven or a deep skillet and brown the onion over medium heat, about 10 minutes, stirring occasionally. Add the beef, stirring occasionally to break up the grind. While the meat browns, drain all but ½ cup of the liquid from the chiles and garlic. Transfer the softened chiles, garlic, and remaining liquid to a blender or a food processor, and process for a few seconds until smooth. Add the chile mixture to the beef, and stir well. Add the crushed tomatoes, paprika, cumin, oregano, and salt, stirring well. Increase the heat to medium-high and bring to a low boil for 3 to 4 minutes, then decrease to a simmer. Cover and cook slowly for 2 to 3 hours, stirring occasionally. Serve the chili warm with tortilla chips, grated cheese, and salsa.

You can substitute a very lean ground beef or ground bison, if available.

THE COWBOY WAY

When you sit down with John, you'll find out pretty quickly that he likes to talk about his cutting horses and his livestock. He tells a funny story about how a female longhorn went off and mated with one of his buffalo bulls. Well, the mixed-breed offspring and the wayward mother were ostracized by the other cattle for a while, and that upset some of the city-slicker visitors. But eventually the fuzzy-headed calf, named Curly, finally got accepted by the longhorn herd, and the mama longhorn was soon attracting male suitors again. That's nature on the ranch.

BRUNCH CASSEROLE

SERVES 12 TO 15

You've never had a brunch dish any richer than this one! Be careful, because once you make it, your family will want it every weekend.

18 eggs, beaten

¼ cup unsalted butter, melted

1 cup sour cream or Mexican crema

1 cup milk

2 teaspoons salt

¼ cup chopped green onions

2 cups grated pepper Jack cheese

½ cup crumbled queso fresco

Taunia's Salsa (page 156), for serving

Preheat the oven to 350°F. In a large bowl, combine the eggs, melted butter, sour cream, milk, salt, and green onions. Stir well and transfer to a buttered 9 by 13-inch casserole dish and bake for 25 minutes. Cover the casserole with the Jack cheese and bake for 10 to 15 minutes longer, or until puffed and browned. Remove from the oven and allow to cool for 5 minutes. Top with the queso fresco and serve with Taunia's Salsa.

CORN CASSEROLE

SERVES 8 TO 10

Taunia's mom came up with this side dish, and it's one of the most requested items Taunia makes at the ranch. You may want to double the recipe, because everyone always wants a second helping.

1 (15-ounce) can creamed corn

1 (15-ounce) can whole kernel corn, undrained

2 eggs, beaten

2 tablespoons sugar

⅓ cup corn bread mix (from package)

¼ cup unsalted butter, melted

2 jalapeños, stemmed, seeded, and minced

1 cup grated sharp cheddar cheese, divided

Preheat the oven to 350°F. Stir the corn, eggs, sugar, corn bread mix, melted butter, jalapeños, and ½ cup of the cheese together in a large bowl. Transfer the mixture to a buttered 8 by 8-inch baking pan. Bake for 40 minutes; sprinkle the remaining ½ cup of cheese on top and bake for 20 minutes longer. Allow to cool for 5 minutes before serving.

BRAZOS BERRY CREAM PIE

SERVES 8 TO 10

One of the many agricultural developments at Texas A&M University, which is not very far from the Elicks' ranch, is the Brazos berry, a special variety of a blackberry. If you can't find these, you can substitute plump, sweet blackberries.

CRUST

1⅓ cups all-purpose flour

½ teaspoon kosher salt

½ cup unsalted butter, cut into small pieces

3 tablespoons ice water

FILLING

2 cups Brazos berries

1½ cups sugar

2 eggs, beaten

¼ cup all-purpose flour

½ cup sour cream

1 teaspoon vanilla extract

TOPPING

½ cup all-purpose flour

½ cup sugar

¼ cup unsalted butter

Whipped cream

To make the pie crust, combine the flour and salt in a mixing bowl and cut in the butter with a pastry cutter, mixing until the dough resembles a small-pea texture. Add the ice water and combine with a fork. Work the dough into a ball, then flatten it into a 4-inch-wide circle. Wrap in plastic wrap and refrigerate for about 30 minutes. On a lightly floured surface, roll the dough out to form a 12-inch circle. Transfer to a pie plate for filling and baking.

Preheat the oven to 350°F. To make the filling, place the berries into the pie shell. In a medium bowl, combine the sugar, eggs, flour, sour cream, and vanilla, and pour over the berries in the crust.

To make the topping, mix the flour, sugar, and butter together in a bowl with a fork. Sprinkle the topping over the filled pie.

Bake the pie for approximately 45 minutes. The filling should be set, but not quite firm. Remove from the oven and allow to cool for 15 minutes before slicing. Top with whipped cream.

BARBECUE IN THE HEARTLAND

KANSAS CITY, MISSOURI

COMING FROM TEXAS, IT WAS HARD TO THINK ABOUT GETTING A BARBECUE EDUCATION SOMEPLACE ELSE. BUT KANSAS CITY IS NICKNAMED "COWTOWN," JUST LIKE MY HOMETOWN OF FORT WORTH, THANKS TO A SIMILARLY RICH CATTLE-BUSINESS AND BEEF-EATING LEGACY, AND I FOUND OUT JUST HOW VERSATILE THE MOST POPULAR COWBOY FOOD OF ALL TIME—BARBECUE—REALLY IS.

In Kansas City, they say that if it moves, they can barbecue it. There's more than beef and pork and chicken; there's lamb and wild game, too, and those are things cowboys have been roasting over a fire since well before the days of the cattle drives from Texas through the Great Plains.

I think what impressed me most is that KC doesn't just have good barbecue joints—it has a wagonload of barbecue experts ready to saddle up and show you the ropes. Everybody barbecues in their backyards and everyone who lives there goes out to eat barbecue at least once a week. And that's not all: Carolyn Wells, head of the Kansas City Barbecue Society, says that this city is the melting pot of barbecue because it is the place where the regional styles from all over America come together. Carolyn also points out that barbecue is so widely popular because it "crosses all racial, ethnic, economic, and gender lines."

. . . THIS CITY IS THE MELTING POT OF BARBECUE BECAUSE IT IS THE PLACE WHERE THE REGIONAL STYLES FROM ALL OVER AMERICA COME TOGETHER.

You definitely don't need a ranch connection to be a good barbecue chef: The Kansas City Barbecue Society sanctions 300 barbecue cook-offs each year, with events that stretch across the country from Vermont to California and down to Florida. And every year during October and November, Kansas City's historic Stockyards in the River Bottoms District hosts the American Royal, a landmark livestock show and pro rodeo event with roots dating from 1899. During the show, the American Royal Barbecue, now ranking as the world's largest barbecue contest, brings more than 70,000 people to town to cook and taste competition barbecue.

What makes Kansas City barbecue most different from other kinds has to do with the sauce. The sauce, I found out, comes in more varieties than you can count. When you go into a Kansas City grocery store, the barbecue sauce aisle is like the salsa aisle in Texas, with hundreds of choices. At KC barbecue joints, it's not strange to find three or five (or even more!) different kinds of sauces. Arthur Bryant's Barbeque, the oldest in town, and Kansas City favorites Gates Bar-B-Q and Fiorella's Jack Stack Barbecue all sell their sauces in stores and online, too.

They say that KC has the most barbecue restaurants per capita in the nation, as there are more than 100 of 'em around town. One of the most popular

is Arthur Bryant's, a landmark place in the 18th and Vine Historic Jazz District, a neighborhood with incredible African-American heritage. Founded in the 1920s, Arthur Bryant's is the place that food writer Calvin Trillin said was the best restaurant in the world. You can't go to this joint without getting the beef-and-fries, a three-inch-high layer of tender beef brisket (check out that great rosy smoke ring!) between pieces of Wonder Bread, with a mountain of lard-fried French fries on the side. At Arthur Bryant's, the original sauce is heavy on paprika flavor. You'll want to get some to take home.

The KC barbecue pit masters welcomed this cowboy hat–wearing cook into their kitchens and generously showed me the art of turning the racks of ribs. They taught me that you don't have to be a cowpoke to produce hundreds of pounds of excellent barbecue every day–but I still think it helps just a little. You might be convinced when you've tasted the Jack Stack Denver Lamb Ribs, Hickory Pit Beans, Cheesy Corn Bake, and Spicy Barbecue Sauce in this chapter.

CHEESY CORN BAKE

SERVES 10 TO 12

This is the best-selling of all side dishes at Fiorella's Jack Stack in Kansas City. It's rich, thanks to the combination of cheeses and smoked ham. Best of all, it's easy to make at home.

2 tablespoons unsalted butter

4 teaspoons all-purpose flour

⅛ teaspoon garlic powder

¾ cup 2% milk

1 (3-ounce) package cream cheese, cut into 1-inch cubes

1 (6-ounce) jar sharp cheddar cheese sauce

3 (10-ounce) packages frozen whole kernel corn, thawed

3 ounces smoked ham, cut into ¼-inch dice

Preheat the oven to 350°F and butter a 2-quart casserole dish. In a 4-quart saucepan, melt the butter over medium heat. Stir in the flour and garlic powder. Add the milk, cream cheese, and cheddar cheese sauce. Cook, stirring constantly to prevent scorching, until thickened and bubbly. Stir in the corn and ham. Transfer the mixture to the prepared casserole dish. Bake for 45 minutes, or until bubbling hot.

MISSISSIPPI DELTA COLESLAW

SERVES 15

This recipe comes courtesy of the Kansas City Barbeque Society Cookbook *and was originally from Skip Gigliotti. Skip's competition barbecue team is the Crispy Critters, a team with members from seven states. The Crispy Critters compete on the Kansas City Barbeque Society and the Memphis in May circuits.*

1 large head green cabbage, shredded or sliced very thin

2 medium onions, sliced thin, separated into rings

2 green bell peppers, sliced into thin strips

1 cup sugar

½ cup vegetable oil

¾ cup white vinegar

Salt and freshly ground black pepper

Place the cabbage in a large bowl. Layer the onions and bell peppers over the cabbage and sprinkle with the sugar. Drizzle with the oil and vinegar. Refrigerate, covered, for 2 to 8 hours. Add the seasonings and toss just before serving.

OLD COUNTRY POTATO SALAD

SERVES 12

This is another recipe generously donated by Carolyn Wells of the Kansas City Barbeque Society from its cookbook. The recipe is one that Ginger Stephens entered to win the first annual Yellow Daisy Great American Potato Salad Contest in Stone Mountain, Georgia.

6 medium potatoes, peeled, cubed, and cooked

5 hard-boiled eggs, chopped

2 large dill pickles, chopped

4 sweet pickles, chopped

1 medium yellow onion, chopped

½ cup sliced green olives

1½ cups mayonnaise

2 tablespoons Dijon mustard

1 tablespoon prepared yellow mustard

1 teaspoon freshly squeezed lemon juice

1 teaspoon freshly ground black pepper

1 teaspoon dried dill

Salt

3 hard-boiled eggs, cut into wedges, for garnish

Paprika, for garnish

Combine the potatoes, chopped eggs, pickles, onion, and olives in a large bowl. Mix gently. In a separate bowl, combine the mayonnaise, mustards, lemon juice, pepper, and dill, stirring to mix. Pour the mayo/mustard dressing over the potato mixture and stir to combine; add salt to taste. Spoon the potato salad into a serving dish. Garnish with the egg wedges and paprika. Refrigerate, covered, until serving time.

ARNOLD PALMER

SERVES 8

It's easy to see why this drink is so popular. Its tart/sweet flavor goes right along with eating smoky, spicy barbecue like brisket and ribs. It's named for the famous golfer, who is credited with coming up with the simple combination of lemonade and iced tea.

½ cup sugar

½ cup plus 4 cups cold water

6 lemons

4 cups freshly brewed iced tea

Lemon slices, for garnish

To make the lemonade, combine the sugar and ½ cup of the water in a saucepan over low heat, stirring until the sugar dissolves. Set aside to cool. Meanwhile, juice the lemons. Combine the juice and the sugar water with the remaining 4 cups water and refrigerate for 1 hour.

To make the tea, steep 4 to 6 plain tea bags in hot water (make it as strong as you like). Allow to cool completely, then refrigerate for 1 hour.

Combine the lemonade and tea in a pitcher. Pour into tumblers filled with ice and garnish with lemon slices.

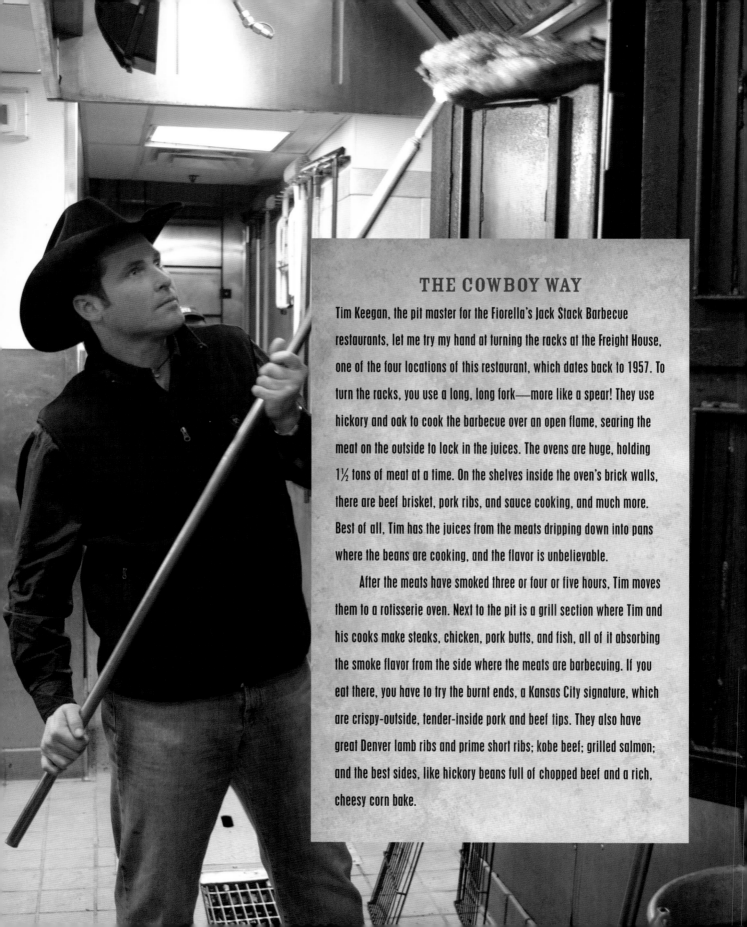

THE COWBOY WAY

Tim Keegan, the pit master for the Fiorella's Jack Stack Barbecue restaurants, let me try my hand at turning the racks at the Freight House, one of the four locations of this restaurant, which dates back to 1957. To turn the racks, you use a long, long fork—more like a spear! They use hickory and oak to cook the barbecue over an open flame, searing the meat on the outside to lock in the juices. The ovens are huge, holding 1½ tons of meat at a time. On the shelves inside the oven's brick walls, there are beef brisket, pork ribs, and sauce cooking, and much more. Best of all, Tim has the juices from the meats dripping down into pans where the beans are cooking, and the flavor is unbelievable.

After the meats have smoked three or four or five hours, Tim moves them to a rotisserie oven. Next to the pit is a grill section where Tim and his cooks make steaks, chicken, pork butts, and fish, all of it absorbing the smoke flavor from the side where the meats are barbecuing. If you eat there, you have to try the burnt ends, a Kansas City signature, which are crispy-outside, tender-inside pork and beef tips. They also have great Denver lamb ribs and prime short ribs; kobe beef; grilled salmon; and the best sides, like hickory beans full of chopped beef and a rich, cheesy corn bake.

HICKORY PIT BEANS

SERVES 10 TO 12

If you go to Fiorella's Jack Stack in Kansas City, you gotta have these incredible beans! The pit cooks get all their amazing flavor by letting the cooking meats' juices drip down into the pans of beans. You might not be able to do that, but this recipe, with brisket, bottled smoke flavoring, and your favorite barbecue sauce, will get you close. This works great on a grill, too; keep your pan of beans uncovered so the grill flavor can soak in.

1 (32-ounce) can pork and beans

1 cup Jack Stack Original Barbecue Sauce or
    your favorite barbecue sauce

1 cup smoked beef brisket, cut into
    ¼-inch dice

½ cup ketchup

½ cup water

¼ cup brown sugar

1 teaspoon liquid smoke

In a 4-quart saucepan, combine all the ingredients. Bring the mixture to a boil over medium heat, and then decrease the heat to a simmer. Cook for about 20 minutes, or until the beans have a thick, soupy consistency. Serve hot.

JACK STACK DENVER LAMB RIBS

SERVES 4 TO 6

Lamb ribs aren't too well known, but they're sure popular in Kansas City. Ask your butcher for spring lamb (less than nine months old) and have him prepare slabs of about 7 to 8 ribs per slab, each slab 1 to 2 pounds. That's what's known as a Denver cut. Serve these with spicy barbecue sauce and Mississippi Delta Coleslaw (page 175).

4 slabs Denver-cut lamb spare ribs

4 teaspoons Jack Stack Meat & Poultry Rub or your favorite rub

If the lamb is frozen, thaw it completely. Prepare your grill to medium-high heat. Lightly season the meat side of each slab with 1 teaspoon of the rub. Place the slabs, meat side down, on the grill directly over a hickory or charcoal fire or on a gas grill with soaked hickory chips. Sear the meat side only until golden brown, about 10 minutes.

Remove the ribs from the direct heat and place on a cooler spot on the grill to finish cooking. If you have one, you could also place the ribs in a slow smoker or rotisserie oven now. Finish cooking the ribs at 260°F for about 1 hour and 20 minutes. Lamb ribs are ready when they reach an internal temperature of about 180°F degrees and you can easily push a finger through the meat of the thickest part of the slab. When they're done, transfer the ribs to a sheet pan or plate; arrange them in a single layer and allow to cool. Serve with Jack Stack Barbecue Spicy Sauce, your local favorite, or try the next recipe on for size.

SPICY BARBECUE SAUCE

MAKES 3 CUPS

This is a great barbecue sauce if you like a good balance of spicy, tart, and sweet. It's not too thick, and it goes well with lamb, pork ribs, beef brisket, chicken, and sausage. Double the recipe if you're feeding a crowd! This sauce will keep in the refrigerator in an airtight jar for 3 days.

1 (20-ounce can) tomato sauce

⅓ cup vinegar

1 to 2 tablespoons molasses

¼ cup minced yellow onion

2 tablespoons paprika

1 tablespoon Worcestershire sauce

2 teaspoons finely ground dried red chiles (seeds removed)

1 teaspoon dry mustard

1 teaspoon kosher salt

1 teaspoon ground cumin

Combine all the ingredients in a medium saucepan over medium heat, stirring well for about 5 minutes. Decrease the heat and cover, simmering for about 30 minutes, stirring occasionally. Remove from the heat and allow to stand for 20 minutes or so before serving.

THE COWBOY WAY

When you pull up to a Gates Bar-B-Q (you can choose from six of 'em), you'll catch the wood-smoke aroma before you get out of your car. Gates does really, really good hickory-smoked lamb ribs, covered in that classic sauce. You have to get the Yammer, a baby sweet potato pie, too. The staff is just as memorable as the food, because they are trained in the Gates family's impressive personal way. You'll be enthusiastically greeted with more than a couple of "Hi, may I help you?"s, and while you're there, you'll want for nothing.

I went to one of the restaurants to meet Brian Channel, a thirty-year veteran, and the last of the Gates' original cooks. He and pit cook Phillip Franklin showed me how to work their pit, spearing and turning racks of ribs in a huge oven where there's usually 1,500 pounds of meat at once—ribs, beef, turkey, ham, chicken, and sausage. On a busy day, they'll feed 500 people in just one of the locations. Mr. Ollie Gates runs the business his dad started in 1946, and he sends employees to Gates' Rib Tech, where they learn the Gates way of making barbecue.

LITTLE YAMMERS

SERVES 12

Baby sweet potato pies are a specialty at Gates Bar-B-Q in Kansas City. Theirs is a secret recipe, but this one should do you just fine. These babies make for easy serving when you're entertaining a crowd, and kids love the small size.

3 medium sweet potatoes, peeled and cubed

1 cup firmly packed dark brown sugar

¼ cup unsalted butter, at room temperature

1½ cups whipping cream

3 eggs, lightly beaten

1½ teaspoons vanilla extract

½ teaspoon salt

1 teaspoon ground cinnamon

1 teaspoon ground nutmeg

1 teaspoon ground cloves

1 package of 2 refrigerated pie crusts, unfold-and-fill variety

Sweetened whipped cream, for serving (optional)

Preheat the oven to 350°F. Place the potatoes in a medium-large saucepan, cover with cold water, and boil over medium heat for 20 minutes or until tender; drain completely, transfer to a large bowl, and mash well. Add the sugar, butter, and cream and use a handheld electric mixer to combine thoroughly to a thick but smooth consistency. Gradually add the eggs, followed by the vanilla, salt, and spices, and mix until blended. Unfold the pie crusts on a floured surface, pressing out any creases with your fingers; use a biscuit cutter or the mouth of a glass jar to cut twelve 3-inch-diameter circles from the crusts. Place these in muffin cups, pushing in to fit snugly; crimp the sides of the pie crusts gently with the tines of a fork. Pour the sweet potato mixture into the mini crusts, until about two-thirds full. Bake for about 25 minutes, or until the pies are set in the center. Allow to cool and serve plain or with sweetened whipped cream.

Gates'
FAMOUS
OL'KENTUCK BAR-B-Q
"HOT LINKS" 60¢
PORK TENDERLOIN
HOT
CHILI

BIG BEND COWBOYS

TAYLOR RANCH

MARFA, TEXAS

FOR ME, THE MOST SPECIAL PLACE IN TEXAS IS A REGION WAY OUT WEST CALLED BIG BEND. IT GETS ITS NAME FROM THE HUGE BIG BEND NATIONAL PARK THAT LOOKS ACROSS THE RIO GRANDE INTO MEXICO, BUT THE WHOLE AREA REACHES FROM MIDLAND-ODESSA WESTWARD TO EL PASO. IT'S ALL BIG OPEN SKY SPREADING OVER THE ROCKY AND FORBIDDING LANDSCAPE OF THE CHIHUAHUAN DESERT WITH MORE THAN 100 PEAKS RISING MORE THAN A MILE FROM FOUR SPECTACULAR MOUNTAIN RANGES.

This is where Spanish explorers wandered hundreds of years ago and where the Cowboy Way lives on as ranchers continue to make a living from their giant herds of beef cattle, rounded up every year in spring and fall as it's been done for well over a century. Big Bend country is a long way from anywhere; mostly you just see mountains and ranch land, and there's a whole lot more cactus and cattle than people.

BIG BEND COUNTRY IS A LONG WAY FROM ANYWHERE; MOSTLY YOU JUST SEE MOUNTAINS AND RANCH LAND, AND THERE'S A WHOLE LOT MORE CACTUS AND CATTLE THAN PEOPLE.

This is also where I learned how to cook, thanks to working cowboy cooks like Guy Lee, who taught me to make camp bread, among many things, and Cliff Teinert, who whips up some of the best biscuits and beans anywhere. In addition to the ranchers, ranch chuck wagon cooks, and cowboys who helped me along when I started cooking at the Gage Hotel in Marathon, there's Louis Lambert, a chef who happens to be a native of these ranch lands.

We worked together at the original Reata Restaurant in Alpine, which is easily one of the most popular towns in Big Bend. Louis trained at the Culinary Institute of America in New York and worked at one of Wolfgang Puck's California restaurants, and he was the first real chef to teach me important techniques in cooking.

Lou, who grew up in Odessa, comes from cattle people; his family still runs a number of cattle ranches across West Texas. Out at his family's Taylor Ranch, located halfway between the Big Bend towns of Marfa and Fort Davis, we got together to make Brown Sugar–Crusted Porterhouse Pork Chops with Apple-Walnut Slaw, Smoke-Braised Short Ribs, Cauliflower Gratin, and Red Chile Grits—some of the goods included in this chapter. We made most of the food on a cool combo grill-and-smoker that Lou designed out of rock; we ate on a patio behind the bunkhouse underneath a night sky that was bright with stars you can only see hundreds of miles from the city.

Even though Lou and I don't work in the ranch business these days, we created a kind of modern cowboy cuisine that paired interesting sauces, herbs, chiles, and vegetables with all kinds of meat, poultry, and fish when we worked together at Reata in Alpine and Fort Worth, and at Fort Worth's Dutch's Hamburgers and Lambert's. You'll find plenty of that in the pages that follow.

186

BROWN SUGAR–CRUSTED PORTERHOUSE PORK CHOPS WITH APPLE WALNUT SLAW

SERVES 6

This pork chop has been a staple on Lou's menus for years. When Lou and I opened the Burning Pear Restaurant in Sugar Land, Texas, this pork chop was voted best pork dish in the Houston area by a local newspaper. What makes it stand out is the combination of the citrus brine and the sweet brown sugar dry rub that develops a crust when grilled over an open fire. To toast the fennel and cumin seeds, use a cast-iron skillet over high heat, shaking the pan frequently and making sure the seeds don't burn.

BRINE

1 gallon water, divided

1 cup kosher salt

4 bay leaves

1 tablespoon coriander seeds, toasted

1 tablespoon fennel seeds, toasted

1 tablespoon whole black peppercorns

½ cup fresh loosely packed thyme leaves, or 2 tablespoons dried thyme

1 cup brown sugar

2 oranges, halved

1 large white onion, cut into thick slices

4 cloves garlic, crushed

6 (12-ounce) porterhouse pork chops

To make the brine, in a large, deep pot, bring 4 cups of the water to a simmer and add the salt, bay leaves, coriander seeds, fennel seeds, black pepper, thyme, and sugar. Whisk and simmer for about 1 minute, or until the salt has dissolved. Add the oranges, onion, garlic, and remaining 3 quarts water. Remove from the heat and cool the brine.

Add the pork chops to the brine and place a plate on top of the chops to keep them submerged. Place the pot in the refrigerator for 6 to 8 hours. While the chops are brining, make the Apple-Walnut Slaw (page 191). Remove the chops from the brine, scrape off any of the spices, and pat dry. Discard the brine and place the chops on a plate. Cover them with plastic wrap and refrigerate until you are ready to grill.

RUB

¼ cup brown sugar

2 teaspoons kosher salt

1 tablespoon ground black pepper

1 tablespoon paprika

1 tablespoon chili powder

1 tablespoon coriander seeds, toasted and ground

1 tablespoon fennel seeds, toasted and ground

To make the rub, mix all of the ingredients together in a small bowl. Prepare your gas or charcoal grill to medium-high heat, and coat the brined chops in the rub.

Grill the pork chops on each side for 3 to 4 minutes, or until the internal temperature registers 170°F. Make sure the chops aren't too close to the coals, as the brown sugar can cause a flame to flare. Transfer the pork chops to a plate and allow them to rest for at least 5 minutes. Serve the pork chops with the Apple-Walnut Slaw.

APPLE-WALNUT SLAW

4 Granny Smith apples, cored and julienned

Juice of ½ lemon

1 cup red grapes, halved

½ cup walnut pieces, toasted

3 green onions, green and white parts, finely chopped

2 tablespoons finely chopped flat-leaf parsley

Salt and freshly ground black pepper

½ cup creamy blue cheese salad dressing

Toss the apples with the fresh lemon juice so the apples don't turn brown. Mix all of the remaining ingredients together with the apples in a large mixing bowl, adjusting the seasonings to taste. Cover and keep refrigerated until ready to serve.

THE COWBOY WAY

Lou Lambert has some of the deepest roots any Texan can claim: He's a descendent of one of Stephen F. Austin's famous first 300 families that came to settle in Austin's original Texas colony in 1829. Lou's great-great-grandfather Joseph McKnight was among settlers who came from Tennessee just after the Civil War to build a new life. The McKnight family is famous through West Texas for its ranching heritage, with a substantial place in the Hereford and Angus cattle ranching business. The first family ranch at Crane is still in operation, and more than a half dozen of their other ranches are scattered through the region.

SMOKE-BRAISED SHORT RIBS

SERVES 8 TO 10

This rib recipe combines two of our favorite cooking techniques, smoking and braising. The trick is to keep your barbecue pit at a constant medium temperature of about 325°F. To do this, Lou keeps a second pit or firebox going nearby to burn oak logs down to coals so that he can simply add these wood coals to the pit while he slow-smokes or braises in the pit. If you don't have time to tend a fire pit, Lou says to just cook these "bad boys" in your oven and enjoy the tender richness of properly braised beef short ribs; they won't be smoky, but they'll still be incredibly good. Most beef short ribs have about 8-inch rib bones. Tell your butcher that you want him to cut the slabs of ribs down the middle for slabs with about 4-inch rib bones.

¼ cup brown sugar

¼ cup chili powder

2 tablespoons kosher salt

2 tablespoons freshly ground black pepper

1 tablespoon ground coffee

6 pounds beef short ribs, cut in half

¼ cup olive oil

2 medium yellow onions, coarsely chopped

6 stalks celery, coarsely chopped

4 large carrots, peeled and coarsely chopped

8 cloves garlic, coarsely chopped

5 Roma tomatoes, coarsely chopped

3 (12-ounce) bottles amber beer

To make the rub, combine the brown sugar, chili powder, salt, pepper, and ground coffee in a bowl; set aside 2 tablespoons for later use. Liberally season the ribs with the rub and allow to sit for 15 to 30 minutes before cooking.

Prepare a gas or charcoal grill. Over a hot fire, sear the seasoned ribs on each side, about 2 minutes, or until crispy and golden. Set aside.

Prepare a smoker or preheat the oven to 325°F. In a large Dutch oven or heavy soup pot, heat the olive oil over medium-high heat on the stovetop. Add the onions, celery, carrots, and garlic, and stir until the vegetables soften just slightly and have a little color. Add the tomatoes and stir. Add the ribs to the pot and push them into the vegetables. Sprinkle the reserved 2 tablespoons of the rub into the pot and pour the beer over the mixture. Bring to a simmer. Place the pot in the smoker or the oven and cook, uncovered, for 4 to 5 hours, stirring every 45 minutes to an hour.

If the mixture becomes dry or the ribs look really dark, add a little water or simply cover the pot. Cook until fork-tender. Remove from the smoker or oven and allow to cool for 5 minutes. Skim the grease from the meat, transfer the ribs to a serving dish or platter, and pour the vegetables over the meat. Serve.

THE COWBOY WAY

Big Bend National Park covers more than 800,000 acres and is home to mountain lions, black bears, rattlesnakes, roadrunners, and mule deer. Places you'd find around the park include Dugout Wells, Dagger Flats, Hot Springs, and Mariscal Canyon. One of the most popular hikes is on the Lost Mine Trail, a pretty easy five-mile hike that takes you on a slow ascent of 1,000 feet. Up in the park's Chisos Basin area, the trail gives you views of Casa Grande Peak, Juniper Canyon, and the park's South Rim. You'll see both desert shrub and forest, with the cooler areas where there's a little shade from piñon trees. If you ever take the trail, you'll want your camera for the good shots you can get from rock outcroppings along the way.

CAULIFLOWER GRATIN

SERVES 8 TO 10

This has become one of the most popular vegetable dishes at Lambert's in Fort Worth. Even folks who don't think they like cauliflower fall in love with this gratin. It's the rich cheese sauce that everyone likes. At Lou's ranch, he made this in a 12-inch cast iron skillet. You can use a deep 9 by 11½-inch baking dish.

2 heads cauliflower

8 cloves garlic, halved

¼ cup olive oil

Salt and freshly ground black pepper

BÉCHAMEL SAUCE

¼ cup unsalted butter

¼ cup all-purpose flour

4 cups milk

Salt and white pepper

Pinch of ground nutmeg

4 ounces cream cheese, at room temperature

4 ounces goat cheese, at room temperature

Pinch of cayenne pepper

½ cup grated Jack or cheddar cheese

Preheat the oven to 400°F and butter a large baking dish. Cut away the leaves and trim the stalks from the cauliflower, cut the vegetable into large chunks, and combine in a large bowl with the garlic and olive oil, tossing to coat well. Transfer the cauliflower to a baking pan, season lightly with salt and pepper, and roast for about 15 minutes, stirring once or twice and cooking to a slightly softened texture. Remove from the oven, transfer to the prepared casserole dish, and set aside while making the béchamel sauce. Decrease the oven temperature to 350°F.

To make the sauce, melt the butter in a large saucepan over medium heat, then stir in the flour. Slowly add the milk, stirring constantly to keep the mixture smooth. Add the salt, white pepper, and nutmeg. Decrease the heat to low and simmer for about 15 minutes, stirring occasionally. Gradually add the cream cheese, goat cheese, and cayenne, and stir until smooth.

Pour the sauce over the cauliflower in the baking dish and toss gently to coat. Bake for 15 minutes; top the baking dish with the grated cheese and bake for 5 minutes longer. Serve hot.

RED CHILE GRITS

SERVES 8 TO 10

Here's a pure comfort dish for Texans and southerners. Lou's mom served grits to their family for breakfast, lunch, and dinner. The ancho chiles in this recipe give the grits an exciting punch, with a flavor that's similar to enchiladas or tamales and works great with grilled pork or beef! Have fun and try this with different cheeses, like cheddar or Jack, or a creamy goat cheese. The puree is good for use in stews, adding to a pot of black beans, mixing into mashed potatoes, and for making an enchilada sauce.

6 cups chicken stock

½ cup finely diced white onion

4 cloves garlic, minced

Salt and freshly ground black pepper

1½ cups dry grits

½ cup ancho puree (recipe follows)

¼ cup unsalted butter

½ cup grated Mexican farm cheese (such as Cotija), divided

Bring the stock to a boil in a large pot. Add the onion, garlic, and salt and pepper. Sprinkle in the grits, stirring. Return to a simmer and cook for 10 to 15 minutes, or until tender. Add the ancho puree, butter, and half the cheese. Stir well. Transfer to a serving bowl and top with the remaining cheese.

ANCHO PUREE

MAKES 1½ CUPS

6 ancho chiles, stemmed and seeded

1 Roma tomato, coarsely chopped

½ cup yellow onion, coarsely chopped

2 cloves garlic, coarsely chopped

1 teaspoon dried oregano

1 teaspoon salt

1 teaspoon freshly ground black pepper

2 cups water

Combine all the ingredients in a small saucepan and bring to a simmer. Simmer for 2 minutes and cover the pan with a tight-fitting lid. Remove from the heat. Allow the chiles and vegetables to steep for at least 15 minutes. Transfer the mixture to a blender or food processor and puree until smooth; you may have to do this in batches. Allow to cool and store in an airtight container in the refrigerator for up to 1 week.

LAMBERT'S CHOPPED SALAD

SERVES 8 TO 10

This is an adaptation of a favorite house salad served at a long-gone steakhouse in Fort Worth. Lou reworked it for the Lambert's Fort Worth menu, and it's a hit. It's quick, it's easy, and it makes a great side for a big, juicy steak, chop, or platter of ribs.

DRESSING

½ cup vegetable oil

4 tablespoons freshly squeezed lemon juice

2 tablespoons white vinegar

3 tablespoons honey

3 or 4 cloves garlic, minced

Salt and freshly ground black pepper

SALAD

1 head romaine lettuce, coarsely chopped

1 head iceberg lettuce, coarsely chopped

¾ cup chopped green onion (green and white parts)

3 tablespoons sesame seeds, toasted

3 tablespoons sliced almonds

½ cup freshly grated Parmesan cheese

Whisk all the dressing ingredients together in a bowl. You may want to adjust the lemon juice and honey to find a balance you like. Set aside and let the flavors blend for at least 30 minutes. At serving time, combine the lettuces and green onions in a salad bowl. Whisk the dressing again well and pour over the salad. Scatter the sesame seeds, almonds, and Parmesan cheese on top. Toss and serve.

ACHIOTE-SEARED CHICKPEAS

SERVES 6

This is a great snack to put out for guests while you get the rest of dinner on the table. It's a big favorite at Lambert's Fort Worth and Lambert's Downtown Barbecue in Austin. Serve with ice-cold beer or a glass of hearty red wine, along with toasted pita bread dusted with cumin. Look for rusty-red annatto seeds in specialty markets or the Latino foods aisle of your grocery store, or order them online (see The Cowboy's Chuck Box, page 207). You can use the leftover achiote oil to rub on pork, steaks, or fish before grilling.

ACHIOTE OIL

1 cup olive oil

2 tablespoons annatto seeds

Place the olive oil and annatto seeds in a blender and process until smooth. Transfer the mixture to a small saucepan over low heat, and heat to about 200ºF, holding the temperature for about 2 minutes. Remove from the heat and allow the seeds to steep in the oil for at least 30 minutes. Strain the oil through a fine-mesh sieve, reserving the oil and discarding the seeds. Store in a jar with an airtight lid at room temperature for up to 5 days.

OVEN-ROASTED TOMATOES

3 Roma tomatoes, halved lengthwise

1 tablespoon olive oil

Kosher salt

Preheat the oven to 225ºF. Place the tomatoes, cut side up, on a baking pan. Lightly sprinkle the tops of the tomatoes with the olive oil and salt. Roast the tomatoes for about 2 hours, or until the tomatoes are lightly browned and most of their liquid has evaporated.

THE COWBOY WAY

Want to get an authentic cowboy look for yourself? You can find lots of nice cowboy gear in Big Bend country. At Big Bend Saddlery in Alpine, you can find everything from belts and buckles to saddles and blankets, spurs, and ropes. They'll even make custom leather briefcases and wallets out of saddle leather, with cool western designs. At the very least, you'll need a good pair of boots and a hat to wear if you're going to take part in a cattle drive, which the public can do twice a year at Big Bend Ranch State Park. You can stay there at the Big House at Sauceda Headquarters or sleep in a rustic bunkhouse. And true to the Cowboy Way, there's usually a campfire at night, complete with guitar-playing cowboys.

CHICKPEAS

2 teaspoons olive oil

2 teaspoons butter

1 medium red onion, cut into 1-inch dice

6 tablespoons achiote oil

2 large cloves garlic, coarsely chopped

3 cups cooked chickpeas

2 tablespoons dark chili powder

Kosher salt and freshly ground black pepper

3 oven-roasted tomatoes, coarsely chopped

Juice of 1 lemon

3 ounces baby arugula

2 teaspoons coarsely chopped fresh oregano

2 teaspoons coarsely chopped flat-leaf parsley

4 ounces goat cheese

Pita bread

In a small skillet, heat the olive oil and butter over medium-high heat. Add the chopped onion and cook, stirring frequently, until the onion is soft. Remove from the heat and set aside. Preheat a large sauté pan over medium-high heat and add the achiote oil. Drop the garlic into the hot oil and swirl the pan; the garlic will begin to color quickly. As soon as the garlic is lightly browned, add the chickpeas and turn the heat to high. Allow the chickpeas to sear in the hot pan for about a minute before stirring, and then continue to cook until you see a little color and the peas begin to sizzle and pop. Stir in the chili powder and lightly season with salt and pepper. Add the roasted tomatoes and sautéed onion and continue to cook to heat through, about 2 minutes. Add the lemon juice and cook for another minute. Remove the pan from the heat and fold in the arugula, oregano, parsley, and half of the goat cheese. Transfer the chickpeas to a serving platter and crumble the remaining goat cheese over the top. Serve with pita bread toasted with olive oil and cumin.

CHOCOLATE PUDDING

SERVES 8 TO 10

Here's a favorite recipe from Lou's grandmother. It's really easy to pull together and keeps well for up to two days, stored in an airtight container in the refrigerator. The creaminess of the pudding and richness of the chocolate are the perfect ending to a casual steak or barbecue dinner.

4 cups milk

1½ cups sugar, divided

½ teaspoon salt

6 tablespoons cornstarch

⅔ cup Dutch-process cocoa powder

8 egg yolks

2 cups heavy cream

1 cup semi sweet chocolate chips

2 tablespoons unsalted butter, at room temperature

2 teaspoons vanilla extract

Whipped cream

Fresh raspberries

Over low heat in a large saucepan, combine the milk, ¾ cup of the sugar, and the salt, stirring well. In a large bowl, combine the remaining ¾ cup sugar, the cornstarch, cocoa, egg yolks, and heavy cream, whisking until smooth. Stir a little of the warm milk mixture into the eggs, then combine the two mixtures in the pot on the stove, stirring well. Continue to whisk the mixture over low heat just until it bubbles slightly, and then for another 30 seconds once the mixture bubbles. Remove from the heat and add the chocolate chips, butter, and vanilla, whisking to combine. When the pudding is smooth, pour it into 8 to 10 small serving dishes, such as custard cups, and cover and refrigerate for about 2 hours or until serving time. Top with fresh whipped cream and fresh raspberries to serve.

THE COWBOY'S CHUCK BOX

GLOSSARY

A

ACHIOTE: (ah-chee-OH-tay) a dark orange-red, sweet and slightly peppery Latin American seed ground into a powder or paste used for flavoring

ADOBO SAUCE: (ah-DOH-boh) a dark chile puree, often from canned chipotle chiles

ANCHO CHILE: (AHN-choh) a dark red, dried poblano chile

B

BÉCHAMEL: (bay-shah-MEHL) a white sauce made with cream or milk

BRAISE: a cooking technique that combines searing and slow-simmering methods to make tender meat

BRINE: a method similar to marinating, in which meat is soaked in a salt solution to preserve moisture during cooking

BURNT ENDS: the flavorful, well-cooked tips of a barbecued brisket

C

CHAROLAIS: (shar-oh-LAY) a breed of beef cattle, originally from France, with a creamy white coat

CHIPOTLE: (chih-POHT-lay) a dried smoked jalapeño, dark brownish-red in color

CHUCK: an old cowboy term for food

COCINERO: (koh-see-NEHR-oh) a Spanish word for chuck wagon or campfire cook; also called Cookie

COTIJA: (koh-TEE-hah) a hard cow's milk cheese, usually crumbled or grated for sprinkling on top of food

CREMA: (KREH-mah) an ingredient similar to sour cream, found in Latino markets

D

DUTCH OVEN: a heavy cooking pot, usually made from cast iron, with a tight-fitting lid

E

ESCABECHE: (es-kah-BEH-cheh) a mixture of pickled vegetables, often spicy with chiles, served as a condiment

G

GAUCHOS: (GOW-chohs) a Spanish term for cowboys from Argentina

GRITS: a starch consisting of coarsely ground corn, usually ground by a stone mill

GRUB: food

H

HOECAKE: a thick, dense bread cooked in oil, similar to hot-water corn bread

K

KOLACHE: (koh-LAH-chee) a Czech specialty, a yeast pastry, usually square in shape and slightly sweet; stuffed with fruit filling or with sausage

KOSHER SALT: coarse salt, preferred for better flavor

KUMQUAT: (KUHM-kwaht) a tiny, orange citrus fruit

L

LIMOUSIN: (lih-MOO-zihn) a breed of large, reddish-gold beef cattle, originating in France

M

MIGAS: (MEE-gahs) Mexican scrambled egg dish, usually made with crispy-fried corn tortilla strips mixed in, typically served with a salsa

MOLE: (MOH-lay) a sauce popular in Mexican cuisine, made in an extensive cooking process involving numerous ingredients, such as chiles, seeds, chocolate, and dried fruits; can be gold, red, green, or brown in color

P

PAN DE CAMPO: (PAHN day KAHM-poh) a flatbread popular in cowboy cooking, usually made in a Dutch oven

PANIOLOS: (PAH-nee-OH-lohs) the cowboys of Hawaii

PICADILLO: (pee-kah-DEE-yoh) a ground beef dish popular in Caribbean and Mexican cooking

PLANTAIN: (PLAHN-tain) a fruit from the Caribbean and Latin America, similar to but larger and greener than the typical banana

POBLANO: (poh-BLAH-noh) a large, dark green chile

POMELO: (pom-EH-loh) a citrus fruit similar to but larger than a grapefruit, with thick skin, grown in Florida but native to Asia

POSYPKA: (poh-SIP-kah) a sweet topping typical in Czech baking, usually found on kolaches

Q

QUESO FRESCO: (KAY-soh FREHS-koh) a Mexican cheese, usually crumbled and somewhat salty, not unlike feta cheese

R

REMOULADE: (ray-muh-LAHD) a mayonnaise-like condiment usually served with fish, occasionally spicy

RUB: a blend of spices rubbed onto meat that forms a flavorful crust during cooking

S

SLIDERS: a trendy term for mini-burgers

SOURDOUGH: a yeast dough that has been leavened with a fermented starter

SPONGE: the warm, fermented sourdough batter

STARTER: the live yeast base for sourdough baking

T

TOMATILLO: (toh-mah-TEE-yoh) a small, green Mexican tomato with a tart flavor

V

VAQUERO: (vah-KEHR-oh) the Spanish name for a cowboy; the word is used also to describe cowboys from Mexico

RESOURCES

ALBERTA CATTLE COMMISSION
(403) 275-4400
www.albertabeef.org

ALBERTA TOURISM
www.discoveralberta.com

ALLEN BROTHERS (prime beef purveyors)
www.allenbrothers.com

AMERICAN LAMB BOARD
www.americanlambboard.org

AMERICAN ROYAL, KANSAS CITY
(816) 221-9800
www.americanroyal.com

ANSON MILLS (purveyors of grits and cornmeal)
(803) 467-4122
www.ansonmills.com

ARTHUR BRYANT'S BARBEQUE
1727 Brooklyn Avenue
Kansas City, Missouri (and two other locations)
(816) 231-1123
www.arthurbryantsbbq.com

ARTISANAL PREMIUM CHEESE (purveyors of Canadian cheeses)
(877) 797-1200
www.artisanalcheese.com

BELLAMY BROTHERS
www.bellamybrothers.com

BIG BEND NATIONAL PARK, TEXAS
(432) 477-2251
www.nps.gov/bibe/

BIG BEND SADDLERY, ALPINE, TEXAS
(800) 634-4502
www.bigbendsaddlery.com

DUDE RANCHERS' ASSOCIATION
www.duderanch.org

DUTCH'S HAMBURGERS
3009 S. University Drive
Fort Worth, Texas
(817) 927-5522
www.dutchshamburgers.com

FESS PARKER WINERY
6200 Foxen Canyon Road
Los Olivos, California
(800) 841-1104
www.fessparker.com

FIORELLA'S JACK STACK BARBECUE
101 West Twenty-second Street
Kansas City, Missouri (and three other locations)
(877) 419-7427
www.jackstackbbq.com

FLORIDA CITRUS GROWERS
www.ultimatecitrus.com

FLORIDA DEPARTMENT OF AGRICULTURE AND CONSUMER SERVICES, SEAFOOD DIVISION
www.fl-seafood.com

FRED'S TEXAS CAFÉ
915 Currie Street
Fort Worth, Texas
(817) 332-0083
www.fredstexascafe.com

GAGE HOTEL
205 North First Street East
Marathon, Texas
(432) 386-4205
www.gagehotel.com

GATES BAR-B-Q
3205 Main Street
Kansas City, Missouri (and five other locations)
(816) 753-0828
www.gatesbbq.com

GRADY'S RESTAURANT
2443 Forest Park Boulevard
Fort Worth, Texas
(817) 922-9980
www.gradysrestaurant.com

HOMEPLACE RANCH, BANFF, ALBERTA, CANADA
(877) 931-3245
www.homeplaceranch.com

KANSAS CITY BARBECUE SOCIETY
11514 Hickman Mills Drive
Kansas City, Missouri
(816) 765-5891
www.kcbs.us

KANSAS CITY CONVENTION AND VISITORS BUREAU
1100 Main Street #2200
Kansas City, Missouri
(816) 221-5242
www.visitkc.com

LAMBERT'S FORT WORTH
2731 White Settlement Road
Fort Worth, Texas
(817) 882-1161
www.lambertsfortworth.com

MEXGROCER.COM
(online store for Mexican food products)
www.mexgrocer.com

**NATIONAL CATTLEMEN'S
BEEF ASSOCIATION**
www.beef.org and www.beefitswhatsfordinner.com

**NATIONAL COWBOY HALL OF FAME
AND WESTERN HERITAGE MUSEUM**
1700 NE Sixty-third Street
Oklahoma City, Oklahoma
(405) 478-2250
www.nationalcowboymuseum.org

**NATIONAL COWGIRL MUSEUM
AND HALL OF FAME**
1720 Gendy Street
Fort Worth, Texas,
(817) 336-4475
www.cowgirl.net

NATIONAL PORK BOARD
www.theotherwhitemeat.com

NEW GRASS BISON CO. (purveyors of bison)
(866) 422-5888
www.newgrassbison.com

PENDERY'S
(online store for chiles, spices, salsas)
(800) 533-1870
www.penderys.com

**PERINI RANCH STEAKHOUSE,
BUFFALO GAP, TEXAS**
(800) 367-1721
www.periniranch.com

RANCHO DE LA OSA, SASABE, ARIZONA
(800) 872-6240
www.ranchodelaosa.com

TEXAS BEEF COUNCIL
www.txbeef.org

TEXAS RANCH LIFE, BELLVILLE, TEXAS
(979) 865-3649
www.texasranchlife.com

VENDING NUT COMPANY
(online store for nuts)
(817) 737-3071
www.vendingnut.com

WILDCATTER RANCH
(888) 462-9277
www.wildcatterranch.com

METRIC CONVERSIONS AND EQUIVALENTS

METRIC CONVERSION FORMULAS

TO CONVERT	MULTIPLY
Ounces to grams	Ounces by 28.35
Pounds to kilograms	Pounds by .454
Teaspoons to milliliters	Teaspoons by 4.93
Tablespoons to milliliters	Tablespoons by 14.79
Fluid ounces to milliliters	Fluid ounces by 29.57
Cups to milliliters	Cups by 236.59
Cups to liters	Cups by .236
Pints to liters	Pints by .473
Quarts to liters	Quarts by .946
Gallons to liters	Gallons by 3.785
Inches to centimeters	Inches by 2.54

APPROXIMATE METRIC EQUIVALENTS

VOLUME

¼ teaspoon	1 milliliter
½ teaspoon	2.5 milliliters
¾ teaspoon	4 milliliters
1 teaspoon	5 milliliters
1¼ teaspoons	6 milliliters
1½ teaspoons	7.5 milliliters
1¾ teaspoons	8.5 milliliters
2 teaspoons	10 milliliters
1 tablespoon (½ fluid ounce)	15 milliliters
2 tablespoons (1 fluid ounce)	30 milliliters
¼ cup	60 milliliters
⅓ cup	80 milliliters
½ cup (4 fluid ounces)	120 milliliters
⅔ cup	160 milliliters
¾ cup	180 milliliters
1 cup (8 fluid ounces)	240 milliliters
1¼ cups	300 milliliters
1½ cups (12 fluid ounces)	360 milliliters
1⅔ cups	400 milliliters
2 cups (1 pint)	460 milliliters
3 cups	700 milliliters
4 cups (1 quart)	0.95 liter
1 quart plus ¼ cup	1 liter
4 quarts (1 gallon)	3.8 liters

WEIGHT

¼ ounce	7 grams
½ ounce	14 grams
¾ ounce	21 grams
1 ounce	28 grams
1¼ ounces	35 grams
1½ ounces	42.5 grams
1⅔ ounces	45 grams
2 ounces	57 grams
3 ounces	85 grams
4 ounces (¼ pound)	113 grams
5 ounces	142 grams
6 ounces	170 grams
7 ounces	198 grams
8 ounces (½ pound)	227 grams
16 ounces (1 pound)	454 grams
35.25 ounces (2.2 pounds)	1 kilogram

LENGTH

⅛ inch	3 millimeters
¼ inch	6 millimeters
½ inch	1¼ centimeters
1 inch	2½ centimeters
2 inches	5 centimeters
2½ inches	6 centimeters
4 inches	10 centimeters
5 inches	13 centimeters
6 inches	15¼ centimeters
12 inches (1 foot)	30 centimeters

COMMON INGREDIENTS AND THEIR APPROXIMATE EQUIVALENTS

1 cup uncooked white rice = 185 grams

1 cup all-purpose flour = 140 grams

1 stick butter (4 ounces • ½ cup • 8 tablespoons) = 110 grams

1 cup butter (8 ounces • 2 sticks • 16 tablespoons) = 220 grams

1 cup brown sugar, firmly packed = 225 grams

1 cup granulated sugar = 200 grams

OVEN TEMPERATURES

To convert Fahrenheit to Celsius, subtract 32 from Fahrenheit, multiply the result by 5, then divide by 9.

DESCRIPTION	FAHRENHEIT	CELSIUS	BRITISH GAS MARK
Very cool	200°	95°	0
Very cool	225°	110°	¼
Very cool	250°	120°	½
Cool	275°	135°	1
Cool	300°	150°	2
Warm	325°	165°	3
Moderate	350°	175°	4
Moderately hot	375°	190°	5
Fairly hot	400°	200°	6
Hot	425°	220°	7
Very hot	450°	230°	8
Very hot	475°	245°	9

Information compiled from a variety of sources, including *Recipes into Type* by Joan Whitman and Dolores Simon (Newton, MA: Biscuit Books, 2000); *The New Food Lover's Companion* by Sharon Tyler Herbst (Hauppauge, NY: Barron's, 1995); and *Rosemary Brown's Big Kitchen Instruction Book* (Kansas City, MO: Andrews McMeel, 1998).

INDEX